# SOCIAL CHOICE
### and
# PUBLIC POLICY

# SOCIAL CHOICE

### and

# PUBLIC POLICY

*Michael <u>Laver</u>*

Basil Blackwell

© Michael Laver 1986

First published 1986

Basil Blackwell Ltd
108 Cowley Road, Oxford OX4 1JF, UK

Basil Blackwell Inc.
432 Park Avenue South, Suite 1505,
New York, NY 10016, USA

*British Library Cataloguing in Publication Data*
Laver, Michael
Social choice & public policy.
1. Social choice
I. Title
302.1′3      HB846.8
ISBN 0-631-14693-8
ISBN 0-631-14694-6 Pbk

*Library of Congress Cataloging in Publication Data*
Laver, Michael, 1949-
Social choice and public policy.
Bibliography: p.
Includes index.
1. Policy sciences—Cross-cultural studies.
2. Evaluation research (Social action programs)
I. Title.
H97.L38      1986      361.6′1      85-18664
ISBN 0-631-14693-8
ISBN 0-631-14694-6 (pbk.)

Typeset by Columns of Reading
Printed in Great Britain by Bell and Bain Ltd., Glasgow

# Contents

# 1

# Introduction

This book deals with two general issues. The first is the way in which public policy on the same basic matters differs from society to society. The second concerns the different types of public response that are often produced by different types of policy area within a single society.

Consider differences between societies. Health, education and welfare policy, for example, differ an enormous amount as we move from system to system. In some societies they are almost exclusively the preserve of the state. The state's general role is barely questioned and public debate concerns precisely *what* the state ought to be doing in these matters, not *whether* the state ought to be involved in them at all. In other societies there is an extensive private market in health and education. The state provides no more than a 'safety net' for the needy or the unlucky. Elsewhere again, these important policy areas lie at the very centre of public debate. There are bitter confrontations between those who want to provide the relevant services via the public sector and those who prefer the private sector. Such confrontations often constitute the red meat of politics. Indeed, one of the best ways to locate people on the traditional left-right ideological spectrum is to look at the role that they advocate for the state in matters such as health, education and welfare. This is because there are important public *and* private components to the value of such services, and because the precise trade-off that a person makes between these is a product of her ideological viewpoint.

The public treatment of many other policy areas often differs rather less, in broad terms, from society to society. Nearly everyone the world over, for example, accepts that defence policy is a matter for government. You may be an outright pacifist or the most hawkish of hawks, but there is something in the very nature of national defence that puts it inevitably in the public domain. In the same way, nearly everyone accepts that the time at which a person goes to bed at night is a matter for her and her alone. Even in the most collectivist of societies, a state decree that forced everyone to have their heads on the pillow by 10.00 p.m. would be taken as a most unwelcome and unnecessary invasion of the private domain. Some activities, therefore, are so obviously matters either of purely public or of purely private concern that this particular ideological element in the policy debate is largely missing.

This leads me to the second important element in the argument that I will be putting forward. While differences in the treatment of the same policy area from society to society often depend on broad ideological conceptions of the balance between the public and the private, the different public treatment of different policy areas within the same society can depend on the fact that some activities are *inherently* more public than others.

In short, I shall take inherent differences between services, and differences in social attitudes towards the value of a given service, as two key variables in a framework that should enable me to move a little closer towards a general comparative discussion of policy *outcomes* in different systems.

The example of cable television may illustrate this general approach more clearly. Cable TV has been hailed as a brand new medium of communication. While the basic idea is not particularly new, the economic viability of a full-scale, multi-channel cable network presented policy-makers with an important new problem. Now nothing is more certain than that, in the years to come, public policy on cable TV will differ widely from political system to political system. We already have some idea of what is likely to happen. In the United States the cable carriers (the companies that actually provide the wiring and transmit the signals) are licensed by municipal authorities, such as city councils. In some US cable systems, such as that in New York, the programme content that actually goes out on the cable channels, whether it is soft-core pornography or political propaganda, is left largely to the market.

Yet, as well as the implications for public morality suggested by the actual programme content, the operation of cable TV has other wide-ranging consequences. It is, for example, a competitor for broadcast TV. If the audiences for broadcast TV fall, so will its advertising revenue. If the revenues of TV broadcasting stations fall, so will the quality (or at least the cost) of the programmes that they transmit. Thus cable TV has consequences even for those who make a conscious decision *not* to consume it. These public consequences of a superficially private activity are known as 'externalities', 'external effects' or 'spillovers'. And cultural and ideological attitudes to spillovers vary greatly from social system to social system.

Thus when cable TV loomed on the British horizon, the response of the Government was to set up a commission and to come up with a national policy on the matter. The effects on other broadcasting media *were* considered by this commission, and the policies that it proposed took serious account of them. There were proposals to limit the proportion of imported programmes used, to prohibit exclusive contracts to show major sporting events and so on. Of course, national cable TV policy in Britain was developed by a Conservative Government that was very well disposed towards the private sector. Its policy was therefore much more oriented towards private enterprise than that which would have been produced by a Labour Government. Yet the key fact is that there was still a *national* policy, while a much wider range of spillovers were at least considered in Britain than were considered, for example, in the United States.

Within the realm of television policy, however, the various goods and services on offer differ in crucially important ways. Broadcast television is available to all who have a television set and is now a vital national medium of communication. Many countries have state-run or state-sponsored broadcasting systems, and they must decide how to raise the money to pay for them. If state broadcasting is funded out of general tax revenue, then all pay regardless of whether or not they use the service. Yet, because almost anyone who wants to receive TV signals can do so and because people watch TV in the privacy of their own homes, it is very difficult to charge people on the basis of *how much* they use the service provided. For the same reasons, people who watch but don't pay must be tracked down and punished by means of a tedious and expensive enforcement process. The problem of paying for public broadcast TV is at least in part a product of the nature of the good itself. With cable TV the signal is fed down a line to each consumer, usage can much more easily be monitored, and the plug can easily be pulled as a penalty for non-payment. New policy options therefore open out. Broadcast and cable TV differ as policy areas, not least because the goods themselves have rather different intrinsic properties.

To summarize the points illustrated by this example, television policy differs *between* societies because there are different cultural attitudes to what is, and what is not, a proper matter for public concern. *Within* a single society inherent differences between different types of television service allow for the development of different policy responses, for example to the problems generated by either cable or broadcast television services.

We will begin the main part of the discussion by looking at the inherent properties of different types of goods and services in some detail, considering in particular the different ways in which people put a value on different goods and services.

We in the West, of course, are heavily conditioned to think of the value of something in terms of the market. What we often forget is that the 'market' is no more than one among many possible mechanisms for putting a value on the purely *private* aspects of a good or service. If I want to sell my rusty old car, for example, I can put an advertisement in the newspaper. I may or may not put a price in that ad, and it is interesting to note that this in itself is a matter that differs between cultures. (You find in England many more prices quoted in the small-ad columns full of cars for sale than you find in their Irish equivalents.) Whether or not I advertise a price, I must settle in my own mind the matter of how much I am prepared to accept for the car. If I fix too high a price, then nobody will buy, and I will be stuck with a car that I want to get rid of. If I ask too little, I will sell easily enough but will be throwing money down the drain, since I could have got more. The market *price* of my car is the one that balances supply and demand. A car that is in short supply – a rare vintage model, for example – will fetch much more than a modern mass-production model. A car in heavy demand (a particularly economical model, for example) will fetch much more than one that nobody wants. Even a rare vintage car would have a very low market price if nobody wanted to own one.

We often equate the market *price* with the *value* of what we are buying or selling. We talk, for example, of vintage cars as being more valuable than others when we really mean that they are more expensive. Yet prices, of course, can be settled by mechanisms quite different from that of the market. Governments can fix prices purely on policy grounds, while monopolists can try to extort high prices for essential goods by refusing to sell unless on their own terms.

More fundamentally, however, the price that is agreed in a particular private transaction is a product only of the *personal* costs and benefits accruing to the actual buyer and seller concerned. My car may have a clapped-out old engine, pumping clouds of noxious exhaust gas into the atmosphere. Of course, the clapped-out old engine will bring down the price that I can charge. Once I have brought the price down and found a buyer, however, we can do a deal. The noxious gases will go on polluting the environment. Many innocent bystanders will go on paying the 'price' of running that car when they breathe the fumes into their lungs, when the sulphur dioxide eats into the masonry of their homes and so on. In short, the used-car market considers only part of the value of the car, that part which is the balance of the private costs and benefits to buyer and seller. It ignores everything else.

There are many additional aspects of value. Cars, for example, clog up the centres of our major towns and cities. They knock down and slaughter innocent pedestrians. They add to the balance of payments deficit by burning imported oil. And countless acres of agricultural land are destroyed to produce the ugly roads that cars need to drive on. Most of these aspects of value are *social* in the sense that they affect society at large rather than those directly involved in the activity concerned. Since the 'free' market can deal only in private costs and benefits, social components of value either must be ignored or must be handled in some other way. Usually the alternative depends upon government action of some sort. We will therefore be looking in some detail at the various possible government responses to this problem of 'market failure'.

The two basic types of response involve the public regulation of private activity and the direct government production of goods and services. Thus a Government could tackle the problem of automobile exhaust either by introducing regulations defining maximum legal levels of various pollutants and by penalizing violators, or by taking over the car market directly, producing and maintaining all cars on the road to acceptable standards.

Whenever Governments regulate or produce they incur direct costs. The funds to pay these must be raised somehow, on the basis of some system of taxation. The notion of 'taxation' must here be seen in its broadest sense. When Governments produce a service and 'sell' this to consumers superficially in the same way as a private monopolist would, they are in fact doing something quite different. Governments can set and enforce prices by *fiat*, and the distinction between a price paid for a service on such terms and a tax is an arbitrary one. Most Governments impose excise *taxes* on intoxicating liquor or gasoline. Some nationalized industries must set *charges* for their services at levels that are fixed by government above those preferred by the management. Good recent examples include 'charges' for North Sea gas imposed by the British Government and those for the telephone service imposed by Telecom Eireann in order to fund unexpected demands for 'dividends' by the Irish Government. Many US local authorities use artificially high 'charges' for public utilities supplied by them as a means of financing local spending. The difference, for example, between a compulsory 'charge' for sewerage or garbage disposal and a property 'tax' from which sewerage and garbage disposal are funded is a difference of name rather than substance.

Whenever and however Governments decide to tax us, taxation creates a whole series of policy problems. Governments must decide whom to tax and how. They may decide to tax only the direct users of the services produced, but they must then identify these users, and this is not always easy. More fundamentally, many who are not *direct* users may still benefit from a given service. (Thus, we all benefit from the education services of the country in which we live whether or not we, or our children, are direct consumers.) Yet if Governments decide to finance services on the basis of *general* taxation, even those who get no benefits must pay. Indeed, even those who deplore the service will be forced to pay, so that someone may be forced to contribute to a new bypass that directs streams of heavy lorries right past her front door even though this road is the worst thing that has ever happened to her. Financing public services from general taxation is therefore bound to cause controversy.

Once a decision has been taken by the state to intervene in a particular policy area, the fact that state activity is inevitably *redistributive* provides another major dimension of conflict. The costs of state activity must be found from within the population, while the benefits will be distributed within the same population. Even if no redistribution is intended, redistribution will be inevitable, since it will be impossible to match costs and benefits precisely.

It is crucial to remember, however, that this redistribution is not merely a product of government activity, as opponents of big government sometimes claim. When I drive my car and pump all of that poison into the atmosphere, I am redistributing from *you* to *me* by making you pay some of the costs of my driving. *Redistribution goes on all the time as an inevitable by-product of every social activity.* Redistribution by government, however, even when it is not explicitly intended, is much easier for people to focus on and attempt to influence; hence it is more controversial.

One of the key aspects of the comparative study of public policy is the attempt to understand why different Governments approach problems of public production, regulation, taxation and redistribution in different ways. The choice between alternative courses of action in a given policy area is heavily conditioned, as I have already indicated, by cultural perceptions of which particular elements of the value of a particular activity ought properly to be considered.

*Any* act, of course, has public consequences. When I decide to stay up drinking and carousing the night before one of my lectures, my students lose. My lecture is a little less brilliant. I may even forget a crucial point as I struggle with my throbbing head. That crucial point might be the one that would have helped students make sense of the course and, if they had made sense of the course, one of them might have gone out and changed the world. Humanity itself might lose out as a result of my night on the town. But I think you would agree (at least I *hope* you would agree) that it is a little far-fetched to expect all of us who teach at universities to be in bed at 10.00 p.m. every night just in case this increases the chance of one of our students changing the world. We all make a cut-off at some point, and we each decide that some of the possible public consequences of private actions are too remote for it to be reasonable to consider them.

People with different cultural backgrounds make this cut-off at different points. Thus, in the United States some would still argue that individuals have a *right* to own firearms. In most European systems *your* ownership of a firearm is considered to pose a sufficient threat to *my* personal safety that it has come to be seen by virtually everyone as a proper matter for public regulation. In the same way, pornography is seen in some cultures as a matter between an individual and her pornographer. In others it is seen either as a threat to 'public decency' or as a degradation of the female sex. In either of the latter cases, the view taken is the result of a cultural willingness to look beyond the individual to broader (if disputed) social consequences.

This book sets out to provide a framework for the comparative study of public services. The framework is constructed on the basis of the general principles that I have just discussed and is intended more as an aid to analysis than as an analysis in itself. One of the main purposes of systematic comparison in the social sciences is to enable us to gain some intellectual leverage on different theoretical approaches to the study of social life. By looking at how things vary and at how they do not vary between cultures, using a set of common yardsticks, we have some hope of forming a judgement about how well the theories fit the facts. This is the problem to which this book is addressed. It is an attempt to provide yardsticks for comparative analysis.

Thus, while I will be using many examples drawn from particular policy problems in particular systems, my intention in this is always to illustrate the principles involved rather than to provide an exhaustive description. Such descriptions are already available, and I shall refer to them where appropriate. This book, in short, is more of an attempt to structure the comparative study of public policy than to engage in it.

# 2

# Why Do We Need Public Policy?

The fundamental problems that create a role for public policy-making are generated by the need for social co-operation, the existence of social conflict and the fact that in many situations it is necessary to reconcile the two. Indeed, it is of the essence of policy-making that it involves resolving the problems produced by the contradictory pressures towards conflict and co-operation felt by both individuals and groups.

Conflict in this context has two distinct types of cause. The first arises from the real or imagined *scarcity* of things that are commonly valued. The second arises from real or imagined *incompatibility* between the goals of two or more people.

The fact that real scarcity generates conflict is so self-evident that the role of 'imagined' scarcity is often overlooked. It may take one of two broad forms. The most obvious of these is created by the consumer panics that begin when people believe that a shortage of some commodity is about to arise. Whether this belief is accurate or not, it is self-fulfilling, since the ensuing panic can quickly clear supermarket shelves and *create* a temporary shortage. This quite often happens, for example, with petrol. The very sight of long queues at filling stations can induce others to queue and fill up. It has also happened with quite improbable commodities such as salt, which no reasonable person could imagine will ever be in short supply.

A more fundamental notion of 'imagined' scarcity arises as a result of the creation of desires among consumers for commodities that they may not 'really' want. This relates to the very complex possibility that people may have a 'false consciousness' of their wants. There used to be, for example, a shortage of blue jeans in the Soviet Union, since these were available only illegally via the black market. The shortage was real in the sense that real people wanted real blue jeans. But did they *really* want them? Or did they only *imagine* that they wanted them because, being unavailable, blue jeans had become a symbol of the forbidden fruits of Western culture? I cannot purport to answer such a question and draw it to your attention simply to make the point that a scarcity arises as a result of a failure of supply to meet demand, while demand may arise for any one of a whole myriad of reasons, most of which are determined socially rather than by basic biological imperatives.

The second cause of conflict concerns the *incompatibility* of the things that people often want to do. When it comes to the process of schooling, for example, it is just not possible to have a streamed and an unstreamed school system at the same time, or simultaneously to teach religious knowledge and not to teach it.

Co-operation is necessary mainly because nobody can go it alone. This is really a matter of *productivity*, since, as Robinson Crusoe found out, it is just about possible to go it alone if by this we mean no more than keeping body and soul together on a warm desert island. Social co-operation yields *huge* gains in productivity, however, and hence huge increases in the general level of social welfare. Allied to this is the problem of co-ordination. Many social interactions, such as ballroom dancing, involve pure co-ordination problems. These are usually situations in which everyone must decide to do the same thing but when nobody much minds which of a range of alternatives is eventually selected.

While nearly all policy problems display a characteristic blend of conflict and co-operation, there is one type of problem that concerns *pure co-ordination*. Obvious examples of it include the setting of common standards, so that plugs fit sockets, nuts fit bolts and we all drive on the same side of the road. In their most extreme form, these problems involve no conflict whatsoever; they simply need a resolution.

Pure co-ordination problems are typically created by some breakdown in, or lack of, communication. When you get separated from a friend in the Saturday-afternoon shopping crush, you each face a co-ordination problem if you want to meet up again. If you both have CB radios and so can communicate with each other, the problem disappears. Otherwise you need a joint policy, which might take the form of the advance fixing of a meeting place in the public bar of the Crane Bar, the Quays or wherever else you both want to be. In large societies communication between everyone is always difficult, so co-ordination policies are always needed.

A set of very obvious examples from the realm of national policy-making concerns broadcasting standards and frequencies. There are several different systems for transmitting colour television pictures, for example. None of us who sit and stare at these pictures on a wet Tuesday evening in November much cares which standard is being used. We don't care whether the signal arrives via the UHF or the VHF frequency bands, or whether the signal is decoded using the PAL system or something else. What we do care about is getting a good picture. This matter is the product of a set of centralized decisions on standards that have been made by the Government. Different decisions could easily have been taken, as we will quickly discover if we take out television set on a foreign holiday and can pick up nothing but snow on every channel. Most of us have little idea of, or interest in, which particular decisions were taken in our own particular system. Provided the co-ordination problem is solved, and we all buy the same sort of set, we're happy. The level of conflict inherent in such policy problems is very low, but they are problems none the less, as we will quickly discover if they remain unsolved.

In reality, of course, a little bit of conflict always sneaks in to most co-ordination problems. For example, there are not enough television broadcasting frequencies to go around. Frequencies must be allocated to broadcasters centrally, to avoid the problems of interference that would arise if people broadcast here, there and everywhere all over the dial. Once this has been done, most of us are mostly happy that chaos has been avoided, though each of us might well wish that certain broadcasters had not been excluded in the process. Whether we crave non-stop, live coverage of amateur angling or in-depth reports on the speeches at local council meetings (or even translations of these into Serbo-Croat), we will each miss something and will have lost out as a result of the scarcity of frequencies. For most people the benefits of co-ordination will overwhelmingly outweigh the costs of abandoning a free-for-all, even if the airwaves can no longer be periodically hijacked by amateur anglers or local councillors. The key point about most practical co-ordination problems is that, for the vast bulk of the population, the need for co-operation swamps any incentive to foment conflict.

## Planning, Research and Innovation Policies

In its very broadest sense, of course, planning can mean almost anything. It includes straightforward but important matters such as making sure that the things that *everyone* acknowledges need to be done are in fact done, and are not done twice. Recent switchovers in Britain and Ireland from town gas to natural gas, for example, have presented very considerable planning problems of this type. Very little conflict is involved, in the sense that nearly everyone agreed on the desirability of the switch. But, given the danger to life and limb of bungling the changeover, huge fleets of vans had to be sent into a particular street on a given day, and everyone in the street was converted at the same time.

There is nothing particularly 'governmental', of course, about complex low-level planning such as this – indeed, gas conversions were often carried out by private contractors.

However, higher-level strategic planning, particularly of the economy, inevitably tends to involve *public* policy considerations. This is partly a matter of incentive and partly a matter of ability. Governments act as very powerful information nodes. They centralize data needed to conduct strategic planning from a wide range of spheres of activity. In addition, of course, no individual private actor, however large or important, would have the incentive to plan across a wide range of activities.

In the same way, research and innovation can often benefit everyone. If we consider the example of research into the cure for an infectious disease to which all are vulnerable, there should be little conflict over the basic need for the research, even though there may well be conflict over precisely how it should be achieved.

Research, of course, can take place at many levels of abstraction, ranging from the solution of very specific and well-defined problems in production engineering to the development of entirely new concepts in energy production or conservation. Ability and willingness to engage in research, which is essentially a speculative activity, tends to depend on the size of the organization concerned. For very large commercial organizations with huge market shares at stake, giant research budgets can be a key factor in retaining market leadership. In addition, as with all risky operations, large scale minimizes the risks and consequences of failure.

Research conducted by major market operators, however, will obviously tend to concern the development of future market opportunities. These will be maximized if the benefits of the research are confined to the producer rather than disseminated widely. An important consequence of this is that research findings, in common with other forms of valuable information, have some peculiar market properties. Such findings, can be withheld from people, of course, and consequently can then be bought and sold on the market. Once they are out in the public domain, however, they cannot be retrieved, and the benefits go to all rather than exclusively to the producer.

The protection of the 'rights' of information producers, using some form of patent or copyright system, has long been a function of government. Thus, if somebody comes up with a major breakthrough in computer technology, she may either patent it or donate it to the public. If she patents it, she will rely upon the effective operation of a government-run enforcement system to maintain her right to sell or license the secrets that she has discovered. Even if government does not actually conduct research directly, it will be indirectly involved in the production of research, if only to protect the rights of private research producers.

There is, however, a key qualitative dimension to research output. Market-oriented research will concern only goods and services that can be marketed. Many research areas will thereby be neglected. One striking example concerns *preventative* medicine. Big companies do extensive research into *curative* medicine, since the drugs and the hardware that are the products of this can be marketed if patents are protected by government. But many of the major advances in modern medicine have been made in the area of prevention. Indeed, it has often been argued that there is only a very tenuous relationship between health and personal (i.e. marketable) health care. The dramatic decline in the death rates attributable to traditional killer diseases has generally occurred *before* specific methods of personal prevention or treatment have been available – by way of vaccination, for example. This is almost certainly true of typhus, whooping cough, scarlet fever and tuberculosis and is probably a product of research-based developments in the sphere of public health and hygiene standards that could not have been marketed by a commercial company.

I will discuss later the controversial link between health and personal health care. For the moment it is sufficient to note that research into public health provisions has been immensely valuable and productive in social terms, yet is an activity that would have been almost inconceivable without a heavy dose of government intervention.

## Policy Responses to Collective-Action Problems

The previous justifications for a policy-making role for government concern circumstances in which the level of conflict is low. When the motives of conflict and co-operation are present in broadly equal measure, however, the nature of the problem becomes quite different.

Returning to the sad story of my elderly car, there can be no doubt that what comes out of its exhaust pipe is no good at all for society. Brain damage, crumbling masonry and dirty washing are all consequences of my selfish desire to drive around in it. The trouble is that each of these evils will continue in full spate if I, *and only I*, stop using my car. There are millions of other rusting heaps of junk being driven around this world, and even new cars are major sources of pollution. Exhaust pollution is caused when large numbers of people use cars, and there is nothing that I, and I alone, can do to stop it. It is therefore a problem of *collective* action.

The example illustrates the three key elements in any collective-action problem. The first is that a number of people cause the problem between them as a consequence of their individual action. The second is that any one person acting individually has an insignificant effect on the problem. The third is that *all* concerned are made *individually* worse off as a result of it. The puzzle is how to bring about the collective action necessary to resolve the problem and make all better off.

Pollution is an absolutely classic example of a problem of collective action. Today it may be car exhausts; fifty years ago it was the coal fires burning in the hearths of most city homes. Everyone wanted her own coal fire. Every coal fire produced smoke, and the combined smoky output of these fires blackened buildings, ate into masonry, dirtied washing and resulted in fog and smog. Eventually, smokeless fuels were invented, but these were more expensive to buy and less convenient to use. For any one person the switch to smokeless fuel was, quite simply, a sacrifice. To expect people to make the change without even a hope, individually, of having a measurable effect on the level of pollution would have been to expect too much. In this case the solution was government regulation – various Clean Air Acts. These resulted in a situation whereby the sacrifices that each was forced to make were made by all and were thus repaid by a dramatic fall in the level of atmospheric pollution. Everyone was better off as a result.

On a global scale, a directly analogous pollution problem now falls on us in the form of acid rain. In this case the actors are Governments, each of which faces the prospect of making huge investments to control power-station emissions, for example, when these often pollute *other countries*. Thus the Irish Government has recently declined to invest the £200 million necessary to purify emissions from its new Moneypoint power-generating complex. This would have resulted in the addition of around 10-15 per cent to Irish electricity prices in exchange for a negligible contribution to solving the problem of acid rain. Yet, if every decision is taken on this basis, acid rain will continue to fall.

The examples discussed above concern one important class of collective-action problem, that of the *public costs* that can arise from the pursuit of *private benefits*. The other main class of collective-action problem is the mirror image of this, concerning actions offering *public benefits* that can be realised only if large numbers of people incur *private costs*. An obvious example is the defence of a country from foreign attack. This is a good that can be achieved only as a result of the physical or financial contribution of large numbers of people. Any one person's contribution is insignificant on its own. The problem that arises is thus one of achieving the public good (in this case defence) as a result of individually insignificant private sacrifices. Each actor knows that, if she withholds her own sacrifice, it won't make any measurable difference to the result.

The major examples of this class of collective-action problem concern projects that involve public investment, particularly investment in aspects of the social or economic infrastructure. Consider the building of a local community centre that would provide a wide range of facilities for a wide range of people. These benefits would be available to individuals as well as to the community as a whole. Yet they would be such that the centre would never pay its way on a commercial basis. Even those who never used the centre, for example, might well value the effects of the social activities that it stimulated. The problem is how to raise the money to build it. If everyone in the community were to contribute £100, the centre would be financed, but each individual contribution of £100 would not make much difference one way or the other. Each individual regards gaining a community centre in exchange for £100 as a good bargain. Yet no one is in a position to do that deal. A Government that produced the centre and levied £100 from each person could give the community what it wants by solving its collective-action problem. All are better off as a result.

The problem of the public costs that arise from actions with private benefits and the problem of failing to achieve public benefits from actions with private costs are analytically identical. Indeed, most real-world examples can be stated either way. Thus, we can see pollution as the public cost of the individual benefits of unrestrained motoring, or we can see clean air as a public benefit arising from the individual sacrifices made by those who restrain their polluting activities. Not having a public good is a public bad, and not having a public bad is a public good. In purely practical terms, however, there is often a distinction between the two classes of collective-action problem. Preventing public bads often involves regulating or restraining individual behaviour, while creating public goods often involves stimulating individuals to act when otherwise they would not. Specific policy responses may thus differ in each case, as we shall see below.

In general, however, collective-action problems run through many of the key areas of public policy-making, ranging from public health to national security, from public transportation to collective bargaining. In each case the policy problem is characterized by a collective need to co-operate compounded by the incentive for each individual to defect from this co-operation.

## Public Policy and Social Welfare

A desire to increase the general level of social welfare runs through many public policy debates. Increasing the size of the cake, of course, reduces overall scarcity and thus *potentially* reduces one of the main forces generating conflict. However, this simple-looking way forward is usually complicated by a series of well-known social phenomena.

The first is that increasing the level of overall welfare may make very few people better off if the increase is unevenly distributed. It may well make many worse off. A system of mass slavery, after all, can seem very productive when measured in terms of *total* welfare. It is thus impossible to separate the level of welfare from its distribution.

The second basic problem with any notion of social welfare is that *different people put different values on the same things*. Let's say that I hate tea and love coffee, while you hate coffee and love tea. If I've already got a cup of tea and you've got a cup of coffee, we do nobody any good if I get more tea and you get more coffee. In fact, we'd do better simply swapping the cups that we already have. In this case social redistribution increases the level of welfare without increasing the size of the overall liquid refreshment budget.

We can think of this as the *qualitative* aspect of the distribution of welfare. It is a particularly important matter, for example, in the field of housing policy. The overall number of houses in a country, considered in relation to the overall population, is a very poor indicator of the level of housing need in that system. People need housing of particular types and in particular locations. Especially in societies such as modern Ireland, with rather high levels of internal migration, it is not much good having thousands of empty houses in depopulating rural areas and thousands of homeless people in expanding cities.

In general terms, housing is the quintessential example of a *qualitative* good. Nearly all of us, save for those who sleep out in the open, have housing of some form or another. A lucky few spend gigantic sums of money in order to put the particular type of roof they want over their heads. The key point is that even in a locality well-supplied with housing *the houses that people want* may well be in short supply.

The most obvious manifestation of this can be found in the long waiting lists of people who want to get out of, or refuse to move into, modern high-density municipal housing developments despite the fact that, in the technical sense, these have all modern conveniences. The quality of life in such developments is seen to be low. This leads people to feel that there is a shortage of *acceptable* housing even when, on paper, there are enough houses to go around. In particular the elderly and families with young children may feel very hard done by, perched on the thirty-first floor of a high rise block. Some improvement, at least, can be obtained by replacing such people with childless couples and young adults, for whom a room with a view and no garden might seem a positive asset. In general terms, *qualitative* redistribution can increase the overall level of welfare without the need to produce more goods.

In the third place, the value that people place on a good depends upon how much they have of it. I might pay you 60p for my first cup of coffee, 30p for my second, 15p for my third, 5p for my fourth – but I might even pay you *not* to have to drink a fifth. When I am so full of coffee that it is running out of my ears, another cup may have a *negative* value. This phenomenon, known to economists as that of 'diminishing marginal utility', is all-pervading. It applies to almost everything, including money. Thus someone on the breadline gets more 'value' out of £20 than does a millionaire. This means that redistributiong wealth *can* increase overall welfare if wealth is taken from those who have a lot of it and given to those who do not.

This is quite different from arguing that redistribution is a good in its own right, to be valued in and for itself. Rather, the argument is that, given a situation in which it is reasonable to suppose diminishing marginal utility, a redistribution from rich to poor may increase the total level of well-being that is actually felt by people, while leaving the overall size of the cake unchanged.

## Public Policy in Situations of Pure Conflict

A social interaction of pure conflict can arise either when there is a cake of absolutely fixed size to be carved up between the participants or when rival participants have incompatible goals. In such circumstances there is no scope for co-operation between the rival parties, since one's gain is the other's loss. Once we get down to specifics, however, there are not that many examples of fixed social cakes. This is because in practice, as we have just seen, different people value the same thing differently and because the value that they put on a given good depends on how much they have of it. In short, because value is subjective, different ways of carving up and distributing the same cake produce different levels of overall welfare. We produce more social welfare by giving the cake in slices to ten people on the point of starvation than we do by giving it all to a millionaire and letting her make herself sick.

Thus, pure conflict in practice arises much more frequently in social life because of the existence of incompatible goals. Very many moral issues, for example, are such that you may decide to do one thing, you made decide to do another, but you cannot do both. You either recognize divorce or you don't. You legalize abortion or homosexual relations or you don't. Such issues, sometimes called 'valence' issues, do not of their nature admit compromise. When people hold different views about them, conflict is likely.

While 'moral' issues, such as abortion, divorce, contraception, homosexual relations and the like tend to provide the classic examples of pure conflict based on the mutually incompatible goals of various groups, decisions over the *location* of activities or investments often have similar properties.

One very obvious example that has recently preoccupied many in the South-East of England concerns the location of airports. Most people probably accept the advice of 'experts' that Britain needs a new airport. Very few people want this airport to be built in their back gardens. Yet the new airport must go somewhere, and there is effectively an interaction of pure conflict over its exact location between different residents' groups in different potential airport sites. The problems of locating new motorways, bypasses and other major roads provide other good examples, as do those of locating rubbish dumps, processing plants for nuclear wastes, glue factories, knackers' yards or indeed any other enterprise from which sensible people like to be as far away as possible.

On the other hand, competition can arise to *attract* activities to a given location. A major new employer, for example, may have decided to locate in one or other of two towns. Intense, even destructive, competition can arise between them to attract the investment and the jobs that will be created. Once more, one's gain will be the other's loss in a situation of almost pure conflict. Yet decisions must still be taken.

There is one major complication in this matter that I will mention only briefly now and return to later. This concerns *logrolling*. When a cluster of valence issues is in the forefront of public debate, and when people feel differently about different issues, a new form of co-operation becomes possible. I may give up my position on an issue about which I feel relatively mildly in exchange for a concession from you on an issue about which I feel strongly. For it to be worthwhile to you, you must have complementary preferences, feeling strongly on my 'weak' issue and mildly on my 'strong' issue. Then we have something to trade. If we both feel strongly but differently on the same issue, then there is little scope for logrolling.

Logrolling has been developed into a fine art in US politics, a system in which the precise location of big, federally funded projects is of major importance. We have just seen that location decisions can generate intense conflicts, but *sets* of location decisions offer considerable scope for logrolling. If we just consider my bridge and your hospital in isolation, we may find ourselves in bitter conflict. If it is simply a matter of who gets the bridge, you'd rather have it for yourself, even though you don't want it all that much. I would feel the same about the hospital. Put the two projects together into a package, however, and we have the chance for me to back your hospital in exchange for your backing of my bridge. We both gain.

This means that the existence of valence issues does not inevitably mean that there will be a situation of pure conflict. There may still be scope for co-operation and compromise over bundles of policy areas, taken together. When there is a single, over-arching valence issue, however, or when all sides feel strongly about the same bundle of issues, then public policy-makers must make decisions in an atmosphere of pure conflict.

## Why We Need Public Policy

We need public policy for all sorts of reasons. The greatest public tragedies would occur if pure co-ordination problems, with no underlying conflict, were not solved. In one sense this is the type of problem that provides the most important – though it is the least controversial – justification for public policy-making. All of the other environments for public policy-making involve the reconciling of diverse pressures towards conflict and co-operation. The simplest version of this problem arises when two groups want to do quite different things, when they must decide to do one thing or the other and when the only pressure towards co-operation arises from the cost of doing nothing. More generally, problems involving redistribution tend to exhibit high levels of conflict, since even quite spectacular increases in social welfare may result from policies that make some people worse off.

The most tantalizing role for public policy, however, arises when the motives of conflict and co-operation are more or less evenly balanced, and particularly in circumstances that have the structure of a collective-action problem. In such cases the actions that are rational for each one of an unco-ordinated group of individuals make all worse off. Different actions make all better off, and the policy problem is to bring these about. I shall give particular attention in the pages that follow to policy problems involving collective action. This is partly because their social character makes them intrinsically interesting, but mainly because specific solutions to collective action problems are particularly likely to vary between cultures and between policy areas.

# 3

# The Role of the Concept of Rationality in Comparative Public Policy Analysis

## The Need for a Yardstick

What we want to do is to compare the solutions adopted by different societies to a range of policy problems. Every society, of course, differs from every other on a whole galaxy of historical, cultural, political and social criteria. It is inevitably the case, therefore, that we will lose a lot of information when we try to make generalizations that apply across a number of societies. The British welfare state is as it is, for example, for all sorts of special, and peculiarly British, reasons that no general framework could ever hope to capture. The role of the Irish Church in education and health policy is in large part a product of the early history of the Irish state. Such problems, however, are faced by all comparative analyses, whether of electoral systems, of revolutions, or of social institutions such as the Church or the family. Yet *systematic* comparison is the only effective way in which we can attempt to hold at least some of the immense variations between societies constant and thereby attempt a logical and coherent analysis of the processes that underlie them all.

All comparisons depend on yardsticks. These enable us to evaluate different parts of the world in the same basic terms. Some yardsticks, such as rulers or money, *measure*. Others, such as colours or the criteria that we use to assess beauty or artistic merit, *describe*. All yardsticks, however, are effective only if they are to a certain extent portable, so that they can be taken from one situation to another and applied in a more or less consistent fashion.

In order to compare policy outcomes in different societies we will need some underlying basis for comparison. One very crude technique that I am using is to concentrate, in the examples discussed throughout this book, on three societies with cultural traditions that are very broadly similar. These are Britain, Ireland and the United States. All possess more or less developed economies; all are more or less electoral democracies; and all have a set of cultural influences that are to some extent distinct from those of continental Europe.

The selection of examples, however, is no more than a first step. The more heroic assumption that I shall be making is that it is possible to evaluate policy outputs as if they were the result of some form of broadly rational process of decision-making. I should immediately make a couple of points for those who are convinced that no decision-making in this world, and in particular no selection of public policies, is rational.

In the first place, by 'broadly rational' I mean no more than that decision-makers make choices in order to fulfil certain general objectives, faced with a certain set of constraints. This does not imply that decisions must be *explicitly or consciously* rational in the sense that decision-makers sit down and carefully calculate the costs and benefits that face them. Nevertheless, it does mean that decisions are the result of *some* sort of cost-benefit calculus, conducted at however intuitive or unconscious a level.

In the second place there is obviously the danger of allowing my broad and generous definition of rationality to be so broad and generous as to explain everything and thereby explain nothing. We will need at some stage to make some general statements about which objectives decision-makers actually set out to fulfil. Such information will help us to explain the different decisions taken by different decision-makers on precisely the same issue. Note, however, that we are not setting out to describe people as rational or not. Rather, we shall be exploring the nature of their rationality, given some basic ideas about their general objectives. As to the constraints on decision-makers, one of the main purposes of this book is to look at the various limitations imposed upon the freedom of decision-makers by the inherent properties of different types of policy problem.

To restate the argument in these terms, different policy problems involve different inherent constraints for decision-makers, and this is one of the matters that we shall be investigating. Different decision-makers have different goals, which produce different policy decisions even under the same set of constraints. The interaction of different types of goal and different types of constraint provides us with a framework, a toolbag of concepts, or at least a language, that we can use to make comparisons, across societies, of the outputs of the public policy process. The idea that underlies this endeavour, however – and I make no bones about this – is that the policy process is in some senses broadly rational.

### Rationality as Cost-Benefit Analysis

Rational policy-making involves the evaluation of policies on the basis of a consistent set of criteria.

Obviously, if we take a number of different policy options and switch from criterion to criterion when evaluating these, then the fact that there is something to be said for almost anything will make it impossible to choose between options. Thus we might favour one project because it reduces unemployment, one because it relieves traffic congestion, one because it helps the balance of payments deficit and yet another because it reduces the level of vandalism. They may all look good in their own terms, but if we've only the money for one, these evaluations won't help us much in deciding how to spend it.

In general terms most of us do, of course, tend to think in this way. Most of us are capable of arguing either for or against a particular project. Indeed, the whole technique of advocacy or debate, including that of public debate, often consists of identifying *non-comparable* criteria that can be used to promote or denigrate particular alternatives. While a lawyer wants to know both the good and the bad points of a client's case, she would be negligent to present these in court with equal weight. She needs to know the bad points so that she is prepared for the worst that the opposition can throw at her. As often as not, however, the jury is asked to weight *conflicting criteria* against one another rather than to weigh different arguments expressed in terms of the *same criterion*. If the latter were the general rule, many more cases would be of the open-and-shut variety.

In this important sense, therefore, effective debate and advocacy are explicitly non-rational. They *disaggregate* decisions into as many diverse criteria as possible. At the decision-making stage, however, the criteria must be weighed against one another, whether by a jury or by anyone else. And to weigh criteria, as to weigh anything else, some common unit of measurement, or at least of description, is needed.

We often dislike trading off two or more quite different criteria in order to make a single decision. This is the same sort of tension as that which a jury might feel when deciding whether to convict or not to convict the man who attacks his daughter's rapist. The jurors' desire to uphold the rule of law and their feelings of empathy (and quite possibly of outright agreement) with the accused conflict directly. This is uncomfortable, and many might wish that they did not have to make the decision. But make it they must, and the only way to do so is to balance the two criteria against one another. Thus we should not confuse the fact that we dislike reducing diverse criteria to a common denominator with the idea that this cannot be done. It *can* be done, and we must do it every day.

Thus after debate comes decision, and rational decisions are taken by evaluating alternatives in terms of common units of analysis. This process is known as cost-benefit analysis, and the following argument is based on the assumption that cost-benefit analysis lies, either implicitly or explicitly, at the heart of public decisions on policy matters.

Cost-benefit analysis is easy to describe in the rather abstract terms that I have just used. It is much harder to put into practice. The basic problem is that there is no obvious or universally accepted common denominator by which to conduct the calculus. Individuals, of course, may be able to balance conflicting criteria intuitively on the basis of the underlying values that they hold, though this process may well be unconscious. Different individuals, however, may well use different criteria, so that the problem of finding a common denominator of value is extremely complex.

Consider money as a denominator of value. An action – let's say, going to university – may have certain financial conse-quences. It may cost money now, yet promise money in the future. Money now, of course, is quite a different thing from money in five years' time. In one sense these are two quite separate criteria. Yet the existence of both borrowing and lending makes it clear that the two criteria *can* be set off against one another. It seems to be the case that people value money in the future rather less than they value money today. People usually demand a greater pay-off next year in order to compensate for a loss this year. The mechanism that is used to link the two cash balances is the interest rate. If I lend you £1 now, I will want more than £1 next year (even disregarding inflation). The fact that people are generally prepared to lend only when real (i.e. inflation-adjusted) interest rates are positive shows that £1 in the hand is worth more to them than £1 in the bank. But the fact that borrowing and lending takes place at all means that people do balance present and future income. Separate criteria they may be, but the interest rate reduces them to a common denominator.

In the same way, the *possibility* of money is not the same as the *certainty* of it. I might offer you a gamble, for example, on the toss of a coin. You give me £1 and call. There is a fifty-fifty chance that you will win £2 and a fifty-fifty chance that you'll win nothing. On balance you're no better and no worse off with the gamble. You may well think, therefore, that there's no point in running a risk of loss for no overall expectation of profit. Yet this would be a very boring way of looking at gambling, and one that would certainly be incomprehensible to the gamblers of this world. And I could certainly increase your winning pay-off to a point at which you'd be delighted to take the gamble. You may not like taking risks, but you can be compensated for doing so.

Return to the decision about whether or not to go to university. This action combines running a risk of long-term loss (you may have a certain job now, but the economy may collapse in three years' time, leaving even graduates unemployable), with the need to set off short-term costs against long-term benefits (whatever the state of the economy, graduates still tend to get better jobs). In order to decide what to do, you need to trade on risk against another, and you need to trade off the present against the future. You will do this when you make your decision, and you could still sit down and work out, given the best information that you can get, whether going to university is a worthwhile investment in terms of the single criterion of money. You could, in short, reduce a limited range of different criteria to the single denominator of 'money in your pocket today' and base a decision on this yardstick.

Another denominator that people frequently use to evaluate actions is time. When working for an exam, for example, you need to put in a certain number of hours of study in order to be reasonably prepared. If the exam is a year hence, you can put in those hours now, next week or next month. You may well value an hour spent in the bar now more than an hour *not* spent in the bar (but spent revising) in a month's time. You may well feel that an hour spent working now will do you less good than one spent working in a few months' time. This happy coincidence of criteria leads you straight to the pub now and straight to the library in the run-up to the exam, and it leaves you on the horns of a dilemma at some point between now and the exam. You can – indeed you must – reduce these different factors to the same underlying denominator (be it revision time or panic) in order to decide whether to go to the library or to the Skeffington Arms at 8 o'clock this evening.

There are, of course, many other denominators of value. These may be ethical, aesthetic, spiritual or anything else. Once we have two, however, we can assess the impact of another serious problem, which is how to reconcile conflicting evaluations expressed in different denominators.

We all know that time is money, or at least we know that this is what they say. In practice, however, we often behave as if this were only partly true. We often do not trade off time against money, at least not in any consistent fashion. We might waste hours saving a few pennies one day, yet squander pounds to spend a few minutes in bed the next. What this means is that the way in which we relate time to money is very complex, but it does not mean that we do not relate them to each other at all.

Most of us will sell a few minutes of our time at the right price. Most will pay something to buy time for ourselves. Thus if you keep offering me more and more work at overtime rates, a point will come at which I will say that enough is enough. I don't really mean that, of course. You could double the rate of pay and I might work a little more, and at certain astronomical rates of pay I'd work until I collapsed with exhaustion. In the same way, some people fork out higher fares to travel on airplanes rather than on trains or boats, presumably because they feel that the time saved is worth paying for.

The crucial point is that, while evaluations of an action or policy may be made in a range of currencies, these currencies can be converted into one another. This means that evaluations can be expressed in terms of a single currency. The single currency that is usually used in discussions of the general principles of cost-benefit analysis is that of 'utility'.

Utility is a nebulous concept that covers many things, but the basic idea behind it is that there is some common denominator that underlies the calculus that people perform whenever they take decisions. Rational decision-making involves the maximization of utility. And the maximization of utility is achieved by performing a cost-benefit calculation that identifies the course of action yielding the greatest expected net utility income.

## Comparing Preferences or Comparing Rationality?

I should make it clear straight away that the view of rational action as utility maximization that I am putting forward here is but one among several that can be found in the literature. I am, in fact, *assuming* that most individual decisions are taken rationally in the very broad sense that I have used the term. Therefore, I am *assuming* that some general form of cost-benefit analysis underlies these decisions. And I am *defining* the concept of utility as the common denominator of value that underlies this calculus.

The main alternative view works in the opposite direction. It begins by assuming that people have preferences that can be expressed in terms of schedules of utilities attached to the various possible outcomes. It then goes on (as I have) to define rational decision-making as the maximization of expected utility income. And the purpose of the endeavour is to investigate the rationality or otherwise of people's decisions in terms of the extent to which the courses of action that they select maximize their utility income, given their assumed preference schedules.

In short, my approach is to investigate the nature of people's utility schedules (in other words, of their preferences), assuming that they take decisions rationally. This is referred to in the literature as the 'revealed-preference' approach. The alternative is to investigate the nature of people's decisions assuming that they value certain things in certain ways. This is referred to as the 'posited-preference' approach. From the perspective of research into comparative public policy outputs, I feel strongly that the revealed-preference approach is the most appropriate. We need to make absolutely monumental assumptions about the different things that people want in different societies in order to conduct a sensible *comparative* analysis of the rationality of public decision-making in different contexts. (And anyway this is probably neither a useful nor, indeed, a meaningful exercise.) It seems to me that it is much more reasonable to assume that different decision-making systems have their own form of rationality and to use comparative analysis to investigate the different types of public and private preference that can be inferred from different policy decisions.

To conclude, I shall be regarding an individual's cost-benefit calculus as the method by which she proceeds to a decision on a course of action, given her various evaluations of the expected consequences of that decision. I shall be assuming that most decisions are made as a result of a conscious or unconscious cost-benefit calculus of this sort. And I shall be using the outputs of these decisions to infer things about valuations that people place on outcomes. The next stage, therefore, is to look in rather more detail at the nature of the cost-benefit calculus conducted by an individual.

# 4

# Cost-Benefit Analysis
# by Individuals

When we take decisions we choose between alternative *actions*. We do not choose the *outcomes* of these actions. Each action has a range of possible outcomes, and it is the actions, not the outcomes, that are within our control.

Thus we can choose very easily to back Speedy Gonzalez to win the 3.30 race at Leopardstown. We can just as easily choose not to make the bet. If we make the bet, Speedy may win the race; sadly, he may not. It is one of those unfortunate features of human existence that we cannot choose which of these two outcomes will take place. We might well *wish* that we could choose to back the winner of the 3.30 at Leopardstown, but wishing, as most punters know to their cost, is not enough.

Furthermore, we may choose only actions that are within our control and capability. Thus I cannot choose to wager £1 million on Speedy's chances at Leopardstown. Neither can I choose that the United States, or the Soviet Union, engage in nuclear disarmament. Nuclear disarmament is an action, but it is not one that *I* can choose.

(As an aside at this point, it is worth noting that the matter of whether or not an action is within someone's control is itself often a matter for heated debate. 'I'd love to tear up that parking ticket, but it's more than my job's worth', 'I'd love to give you a bigger pay rise, but the firm would go bankrupt' are popular refrains that most people have heard at one time or another. A key element in bargaining often involves establishing precisely which actions are in fact open to people.)

The two basic problems, therefore, are to specify the actions that are open to us and to specify the range of outcomes that each action is likely to generate. Having done this, we evaluate each outcome and assess the probability of its occurring. With all of this information we can evaluate the bundle of likely outcomes generated by each action and choose the action that promises the highest utility income.

## Specifying Possible Courses of Action

Decisions often present themselves in a deceptively simple guise. For example, you may be deciding whether or not to buy a new car. If you already have a car, the two courses of action might appear to be:

ACTION 1 ($A_1$)   Keep your old car
ACTION 2 ($A_2$)   Sell your old car and buy a new one (either using up some of your savings or borrowing the money to make up the extra cash that you need).

Of course, there is a whole range of new cars that you could buy, so action 2 is rather more complex than I have represented it to be. The key point, however, is that other, quite different, actions are also open to you. If you keep your old car, for example, you leave your savings intact rather than spending some of them on rusting metal. There is now a whole range of *other* things that you can do with the money. You can take it all out of the bank in cash and back Speedy Gonzalez to win the 3.30 at Leopardstown. At odds of 25-1 you'd be a fair sight richer if he won. You can play the stock market, build an extension to your home, speculate in pork-belly futures or even give all of the money to charity. Each of these options is open to you, along with a nearly infinite number of others.

Specifying all of the options that are open to you in any

given situation would quickly drive you mad – indeed, most people would probably think of this as a form of neurosis. But ignoring all of the options that are open to you is clearly very shortsighted.

Let's say that you must use £5,000 of your own cash to change your car, and let's say that you can buy a gilt-edged, fixed-interest bond that pays 10 per cent per annum. If you put the £5,000 into these bonds rather than into a car dealer's pocket, you will certainly receive £500 each year in interest. One of the costs of running your car, without any doubt at all, is the £500 each year in lost interest on the bonds that you cannot now buy. There is no fancy footwork about this. The £500 a year would be real crinkly notes in your back pocket if you bought the bonds rather than a new car.

While people often forget, or at least try to forget, the 'interest-forgone' cost of tying up their liquid capital in a rusting car, they are not *allowed* to forget the 'interest-payable' cost if they can't or won't tie the capital up and borrow the money instead. The £5,000 worth of capital represented by your new car has to be serviced with interest payments one way or the other. If you borrow the money, you pay the interest directly. If you use your own money, you lose the interest on it that others would pay you.

The costs of opportunities lost are usually referred to as the 'opportunity costs' of the chosen course of action. In very general terms, of course, each action has any number of opportunity costs. To keep things under control, therefore, we usually concentrate on the most profitable and *effectively certain* (legal) opportunity forgone. For the capital costs of an action this is often presented in terms of the best available interest rate on a gilt-edged investment. This is certainly a minimum opportunity cost and one that can be generally applied to a range of individuals in a range of different circumstances.

Opportunities lost, however, present themselves in a range of guises. For people who are working, for example, the opportunity cost of an afternoon's unpaid leave spent happily backing winners at Leopardstown must certainly include lost wages as well as the cost of admission to the racetrack. For a student sinking yet another pint of Guinness in the Skeffington Arms the cost must certainly include another thirty minutes not spent reading some fascinating book on comparative public policy that might help her through her final examinations. In general terms, none the less, there is no doubt about how to specify opportunity costs when at least one alternative course of action yields an outcome that is virtually certain.

There are two ways in which opportunities lost can be included in any decision calculus. A certain option can be selected as a reference point, and the utility income from it can be calculated. Other options can then be evaluated and, if they yield a smaller utility income, the difference between the income they yield and the income from the 'certain' reference option can be included as an opportunity cost.

This is the method used, for example, by the Consumers' Association (CA) in Britain when it compares the cost of running different automobiles. To the total of all other costs, including depreciation on capital, is included a 'capital cost' of owning the car. This is the real cost of capital if the money needed to buy the car must be borrowed. Few could quibble with this, since real pounds must be sent monthly to the finance company to meet the interest charges. Alternatively, it may be an opportunity cost of capital tied up in the car, denominated in terms of interest forgone on the owner's own capital. People who are unwilling to have the full costs of their motoring laid bare may feel that this opportunity cost is in some senses mischieviously applied by the CA in order to exaggerate motoring costs. Yet if they were to sell the car and bank the cash, the interest payments they would receive would also be denominated in real pound notes. Including the opportunity cost of capital employed in car ownership enables comparisons to be made between the overall costs of running cars of different values. The underlying assumption behind this method of taking account of lost opportunities is, of course, that *some car is going to be bought*, and the decision revolves around which precise model it is to be. Actually, *not* owning a car and investing the money instead is not seriously considered as an option by most people. The reference option of the gilt-edged investment is used to highlight the variation between models in one of the best-disguised costs of car ownership.

Another closely analogous situation concerns home ownership. Most home owners are delighted with the way in which their mortgage payments (net of tax relief) depreciate with inflation, usually becoming far lower than current market rents for similar properties. Few take into account the fact that they often have many thousands of their own pounds tied up in their house. They *could* sell the house, bank the money and earn substantial interest payments that would go a long way towards defraying their rent. For someone with £10,000 tied up in a house, who could get 10 per cent interest on her capital, the opportunity cost of home ownership is £1,000 per year. This is to say not that home ownership is not cost-effective but that this particular cost is often ignored. Businesses, on the other hand, often lease cars and plant rather than buy them because they are acutely aware of the alternative opportunities for their capital.

The opportunity-cost method of taking account of opportunities lost tends to be used when a *general* course of action, such as owning a car or a house, has already been selected and the cost-benefit calculus is concerned with selecting the best available option. The alternative method is relevant when decisions are to be taken between general courses of action. Here, the gilt-edged reference option should be included in its own right as a viable option and evaluated alongside the others. Opportunity costs should *not* then be included in the evaluation of other options, otherwise they will be counted twice. If the gilt-edged option yields the highest return, it selection will be indicated by cost-benefit analysis. Only if it is not selected does an opportunity cost arise.

Thus a consumer may be deciding whether to own a car at all. In this case the benefits of car ownership must be set alongside all of the basic costs (ignoring opportunity costs).

The net return can be compared with that of a gilt-edged investment (taking account, of course, of consequent transport costs). The implication is then that a car will *not* be bought if the gilt-edged return is higher.

In short, the point of specifying the widest possible range of options is to identify the opportuities lost as a result of selecting any single option. Lost opportunities must be included in the calculus somewhere. This can be achieved *either* by including the best secure option as a potential real course of action in its own right *or* by using it as a reference point to calculate the relative opportuity costs of real options. To fail to do either is simply to fail to include all of the costs of the range of options open to you.

The selection of gilt-edged options for this purpose, of course, is nothing more than a conservative approximation to the real world. Thus you will not find accountants advising you of the opportunities you are missing at Leopardstown this afternoon when you buy a new car – despite the fact that these are *real* opportunities missed – because it is difficult to generalize from them. This does not detract from the fact that if you know *for certain* that all of the other horses have been nobbled, you should still put your shirt on Speedy Gonzalez to win the 3.30.

Beyond the specification of gilt-edged options, however, it is difficult to generalize about what should be included in a decision calculus in order to capture the full range of actions available to you. Particular individuals, of course, may consider all sorts of bizarre opportunities before making their decision. Understanding the extent of these is part of the process of understanding the rationality of a particular individual's decision. For the purposes of general discussion, however, we can do no more than specify that, at the very least, the best available gilt-edged option should be included in order to provide some (albeit conservative) indication of overall opportunity cost.

## Specifying the Outcomes

As I've mentioned, we choose between *actions*, not *outcomes*. Fate, chance, luck, God and many other forms of contingency intervene to determine the precise outcome of any given action. Thus if I step off the kerb a hundred times without looking for cars, I may well *never* be knocked down and killed. If I look right and left several times before each crossing, it may happen that a maniac speedster with faulty brakes will swoop in out of nowhere and slaughter me. However I step off the kerb, there are at least two possible outcomes – one that I will make it to the other side in one piece, the other that I will not. Notwithstanding such a sobering thought, the fact remains that different actions generate different outcomes at different levels of probability. As we drum into every 3-year-old, looking both ways before you cross, *and* not crossing if there is an approaching car, considerably reduces the *probability* of getting knocked down.

To conduct a perfect cost-benefit analysis, therefore, we should specify every potential outcome of every potential action. In a world in which anything can happen, this in itself would take for ever. Thus we take short cuts. We don't usually consider the possibility of being felled by a giant hailstone every time we step outside the front door, despite the fact that somebody was indeed killed this way in France in June 1984. We ignore many possible outcomes, usually because the probabilities associated with them are minuscule. We do so because conducting a cost-benefit analysis is itself a costly business, at the very least in terms of time and energy spent thinking and because there is no point in devoting a lot of resources to taking the very best decision if the costs of taking this decision outweigh any foreseeable benefits. In so doing we are taking the first step away from the pure maximization of *gross* utility income. We are still maximizing *net* utility income by making the best decision we can, considering all of the costs of decision-making. This process is sometimes known as 'satisficing', as opposed to maximizing.

I have already been involved in a process of surreptitious satisficing when talking about gilt-edged options. Nothing in this life, of course, is certain. When you put your money on deposit with a major bank or buy government bonds, for example, there is a finite, though tiny, chance that either the bank or the Government will go broke. You may indeed lose all of your money with even these gilt-edged investments. To keep matters under control, however, I have ignored such remote possibilities. You could spend a lot of money investigating the chances that the US Government, for example, would not pay out on its bonds. You would have better information at the end of it, perhaps discovering that the probability of this happening was indeed not zero but 0.0000001. But the money that you invest in improving the information on which you base your decision-making would be wasted in the sense that it would have cost you more to gather than you could ever realistically expect to gain as a result of taking a better-informed decision.

Thus we specify the outcomes that it seems worth while to specify. And to decide what it seems worth while to specify we use, if you like, a quick cost-benefit analysis on our cost-benefit analysis. This tends to exclude outcomes that are very remote, though quite *how* remote is 'very' remote will depend on the cost or benefit of the outcome. We might exclude a 1 in 1,000 chance of stubbing a toe when deciding whether to cross a road but count in a 1 in 1,000 chance of meeting our Maker under the wheels of a 10-ton truck.

Satisficing, of course, is very common in real life. When we buy a box of matches, for example, we buy the first box that comes to hand. Only mad people would do extensive market research into which box offers the most matches per penny. Many people walk or drive to work the same way every day, often ignoring possible short cuts because the possible costs of getting lost while exploring them do not seem worth the potential benefits. The precise ways in which a particular individual satisfices is another personal element of her own private system of rationality. In general terms we can do no more than specify that satisficing is undoubtedly more rational than maximizing without taking account of decision costs. Put another way, satisficing *is* maximizing once decision costs are taken into consideration.

## Evaluating Actions

We have already seen that every outcome of any action has a probability, as well as a value, attached to it. We will be returning in subsequent chapters to the various aspects of the value of an outcome. Pretend, for the moment, that we can put a figure on this. Once we have enumerated all of the possible outcomes of an action, we can evaluate the utility income to be expected from the action itself. We do this by adding together the expected value of all possible outcomes associated with it, with each outcome weighted by the probability that it will actually occur.

The classic example of this process is betting. Returning to the tricky problem of what to do about Speedy Gonzalez and the 3.30 at Leopardstown, a bookie may offer to take £10 from me if Speedy loses and to give me £100 if he wins. He is offering me a win-only bet on Speedy Gonzalez at odds of 10–1. Let's assume that I decide to ignore the possibility that the bookie will abscond with my money quite regardless of the outcome of the race. (We're satisficing already, since such sad eventualities are not entirely unheard-of.) If I bet (action $A_1$), there are two outcomes that I need to consider:

$A_1$  $O_1$ Speedy Gonzalez wins the race and I win £100
   $O_2$ Speedy Gonzalez loses the race and I lose £10

If I don't bet (action $A_2$), I may have my pocket picked during the race and lose the £10 anyway. Ignoring this and other disasters, there is only one likely outcome:

$A_2$  $O_1$ I neither win nor lose anything – value £0

Fortunately, action $A_2$ is easy to evaluate, yielding a single outcome with absolute certainty. The value of not betting is £0, and in order to decide whether or not to bet, I must compare this zero pay-off with the expected value of betting (action $A_1$).

The expected value of placing the bet, of course, depends crucially on the probability that Speedy will win the race. If the horse has three legs and no brain, this probability is small. I might as well just give the book-maker £10. If Speedy is the only horse in the race, he will win if he merely avoids falling over. The probability of this is high, and I stand a good chance of making £100.

In general, the greater the chance (the higher the probability) of Speedy's winning, the more valuable the bet looks. In fact, the value of the bet is:

$$(P_1 \times £100) + (P_2 \times (-£10))$$

where $P_1$ is the chance of Speedy's winning and $P_2$ is the chance of his losing. (If we disregard all other possibilities, then $P_1 + P_2 = 1$.)

Thus, if there is no chance of Speedy's winning ($P_1 = 0$), then the value of the bet is $-£10$. (In other words, I'll be giving the bookie £10.) If he is certain to win ($P_2 = 0$), then the value of the bet is £100. (In other words, the bookie will be giving me £100.) If there is a 50-50 chance that Speedy will win ($P_1 = 0.5$, $P_2 = 0.5$), then the value of the bet is £50 + ($-£5$), or £45. (In other words, if I keep doing this over and over again, I'll win some bets and lose some, but *on average* I'll win £45 a time.) If there's a 1 in 11 chance that he'll win ($P_1 = 0.09$, $P_2 = 0.91$), the value of the bet is £9+ ($-£9$), or zero. (If I keep backing Speedy at these odds for ever, I'll neither win nor lose money on balance.)

In other words, making the bet is worth the same as doing nothing if Speedy has a 1 in 11 chance of winning. If he has a better chance, the bet is worth while. If he has a worse chance of winning than 1 in 11, the bet is not worth making. All you have to do (he said with a hollow laugh) is to estimate the probability of the horse's winning the race in order to conduct a cost-benefit analysis and decide whether or not to bet. Because you have to *estimate* the probability of the horse's wining, it is known as a 'subjective probability'. If the probability were fixed and known (as is the case with the probability that a given number or colour will come up on a true roulette wheel), then it would be known as an 'objective probability'.

The fact that you often have to estimate probabilities does not, however, mean that you cannot conduct a rational cost-benefit calculus. You operate with the best information that you can get (by buying a form book, say, or even by listening to hot tips from the horse's mouth – if you trust the source). At least you operate with the best information that it seems worth getting. Once more, accumulating the information necessary to make better estimates of subjective probabilities costs money and time. (You have to pay for all form books and most tips.) There is no point in refining these estimates, at great cost, if the improved estimates make little difference to your conclusion. Once more you satisfice rather than maximize, this time by settling for subjective probabilities that are less accurate than those that you could conceivably discover. But to do so is quite rational once the cost of a cost-benefit calculus is taken into account.

In general terms, you evaluate the expected utility of action $A$ call this $U(A)$ by enumerating and evaluating its likely outcomes (say there are $N$ of these, and call their values $O_{A1}$ to $O_{AN}$) and the probabilities of each of these happening, given action $A$ (call these probabilities $P_{A1}$ to $P_{AN}$, and remember that they will add up to 1). The expected utility of $A$ is the sum of the values of each outcome, weighted by its probability. In other words:

$$U(A) = P_{A1} \, O_{A1} + P_{A2} \, O_{A2} + \ldots + P_{AN} \, O_{AN}$$

The rational decision-maker simply evaluates each of the actions open to her in this way and chooses the one yielding the highest expected utility!

## Probability and Risk

So far I have looked at probabilities in a very neutral way. I have assumed that an action that has a 50 per cent chance of winning you £100 and a 50 per cent chance of losing you £100 has exactly the same expected value as one that promises you precisely nothing.

In reality, of course, some people like taking risks, and some do not. There are people who bet on the colours at roulette, at even odds, despite the fact that they know that the probability of winning is less than even. They presumably do so because they enjoy the process of taking risks and can be thought of as *risk-lovers*. Other people insure themselves against extremely unlikely eventualities (the possibility of the postperson falling over and breaking her leg on their front path, for example) despite the fact they know that, in general, insurance companies make profits out of such business. They are opting not to take a risk even when this option costs money. Presumably they do so because they dislike the taking of risks and can be thought of as *risk-averters*.

Gambling and insurance are classic examples of activities that people who love risk and people who hate it are likely to engage in. Indeed, there is no essential difference between gambling and insurance in this respect. Insuring your car, after all, is rather like making a bet with the insurance company that it will be wrecked at some time during the following year. After the event backed or insured against has not happened, both the gambler and the person taking out insurance may regret her action, since in a sense both the bet and the insurance premium are wasted. Of course, the gambler will tell you that she enjoyed the bet in itself, while the insured person will tell you that she enjoyed the peace of mind. The only difference is that the gambler is laying *on* a risk for herself, while the person taking out insurance is laying *off* the risk on to somebody else.

Before moving on, it is important to note that there are two separate aspects to what we commonly think of as running a risk. There is the process of taking a decision in the light of known, fixed odds (that is, in the knowledge of the objective probabilities). This is what is involved, for example, in betting at roulette or, indeed, at most card games (though much of the skill involved in selecting the maximum-value bet at a game such as poker involves knowing how to calculate very complex objective probabilities). This is a form of decision-making in a situation of certainty, since while the outcomes themselves are not certain, the pay-offs and the probabilities associated with them are.

It is more usually the case, however, that we are forced to take a decision, in a situation of uncertainty, not only about the outcomes of actions but also about the related probabilities and pay-offs. When I bet on a horse race, for example, only God, fate or hindsight can tell me the objective probabilities involved – I must assess these subjectively for myself before I can take action.

In short, there are two types of risk that people take. There are 'certain' risks, and there are 'uncertain' risks, and it is quite possible that people have quite different attitudes to these. Some may be prepared to take a chance at certain odds but not when the probabilities are unknown. Others may derive satisfaction from backing their judgement of the odds and *prefer* to take risks when assessing the subjective probabilities is a matter of skill.

The key point is that risk-taking is not a neutral process and that different attitudes to risk may well lead two decision-makers to choose quite different actions when faced with an identical set of options. Moreover, general cultural attitudes to risk will vary. The dominant ideology in many Western systems seems to be that gambling (on the horses at least, if not on the stock market) is a bad thing and insurance is a good thing. Even within these societies, however, there are major subcultures that regard insurance as a matter for idiots and gambling as quite the thing to do.

## Taking Time into Account

So far we have been talking about evaluating actions as if each outcome were a once-and-for-all affair. If Speedy Gonzalez wins the race, he wins it. I get paid off and that's that. Many actions, however, have outcomes that produce a stream of pay-offs over time. Any decision about a career, for example, concerns a flow of income over a period of years. Some careers yield very low returns at the outset but rapidly rising pay packets over time. Others offer a higher starting salary but little prospect of improvement. Given that people value resources now in a way different from that in which they value resources in the future, as we have seen, we need to know how to put a figure on streams of utility that flow in over a period of time.

It is commonly supposed that most people value future utility rather less than they value present utility. For this reason we usually evaluate future utility by applying what is known as a 'discount rate' to it. For example, if I value income next year at 10 per cent less than I value income now, my discount rate would be 90 per cent or 0.9. (If I happen to value future income at 10 per cent *more* than present income, the discount rate would be 110 per cent or 1.1 – not an entirely implausible possibility.)

The important principle reflected in the discount rate, however, is that it is possible to put a value today on a piece of utility that will actually be enjoyed in the future. This is the *present value* of future utility. If we could not do this, then taking rational decisions today about what might happen in the future would be a difficult process indeed.

Of course, the way in which future utility is discounted will vary immensely between individuals. Most of us have what we can think of as 'time horizons', limits beyond which we will not look at all to the future. Beyond these time horizons we effectively discount future utility to zero. When considering a matter such as the depletion of natural resources, for example, and formulating preferences about alternative courses of action, some people may feel a genuine concern for the welfare of future generations, while others may look no further ahead than a few years. Either way, people are likely to be more concerned about the prospect of the collapse of the world energy system in the year 2000 than about the prospect of its collapse in the year 2222.

When looking at the way in which people evaluate the future we should be careful not to confuse two matters. Future events are less certain, in the sense that the subjective probabilities associated with them are much harder to assess. Some people, for example, might postpone concern about a future energy crisis because they genuinely believe that 'something will turn up' to solve it. Others may be quite certain that an energy crisis will cause the collapse of civilization as we know it within the space of twenty-five years but may simply care very little about anything that might happen so far into the future. The evaluation of future events is affected both by their uncertainty and by their remoteness, and we must take care not to conflate two quite separate effects.

One of the most important aspects of public policy that is affected by time discounting is the process of investment. Whether public or private, since an investment involves the sacrifice of utility in the short term in the expectation of greater utility in the longer term, people's discount rate relates directly to the rate of return that they expect on a 'profitable' investment. Imagine that, viewed from the perspective of today, I regard £100 received next year as being worth only £90 now. If I lend you £90 now, you'll have to give me £100 next year to make it worth my while. This is a rate of return (an interest rate, in this case) of about 11 per cent. If you offer me less than this, I'd prefer to hang on to the £90 that I already have.

The matter of investment nicely illustrates the distinction between the risks and the remoteness of future utility. Some people demand higher rates of return on their investments because they discount future utility more steeply than others. Those, in particular, who are in short-term financial difficulty may look for very high rates of return before they are prepared to commit present cash. A quite separate reason for demanding a higher rate of return concerns the estimated *security* of the investment. Thus government bonds can offer lower interest rates than I will have to offer, for example, if I wish to borrow way over my head in order to finance one of those spectacular betting coups. The risks associated with the betting coup provoke demands for higher rates of return, even from those who are otherwise quite sanguine about future utility income.

An important area of non-market activity in which Governments may get involved concerns the making or the guaranteeing of loans, at normal interest rates, to those who are assessed by market lenders as being too risky. As we shall see, the British and Irish Governments make, and the US Government guarantees, housing loans to those who fail to meet the requirements of the various housing finance institutions. In either case government agencies consciously tolerate a higher level of risk for a given rate of future returns than does a private sector that might well lend to higher risks but only at much higher interest rates.

At the level of individual cost-benefit analyses, attitudes to the future can often be inferred from domestic investment decisions. Continuing within the general area of energy policy, Governments in recent years have gone to some lengths to encourage energy conservation in private homes. They have quantified the rates of return on domestic investment in various forms of home insulation, for example. By now most people know that the cost of lagging an electric hot-water cylinder is paid back in energy savings in about six months. This is a short enough period to represent a rational investment for almost anyone, even a transient apartment-dweller. The insulation of an attic also has a relatively short pay-back period, but the retro-fitting of double glazing, on the other hand, takes over ten years to pay for itself at current prices. The installation of a solar energy system in northern climates takes longer still. We should not expect to see people living in rented apartments rushing to install double glazing. Indeed, when we see someone installing double glazing on energy-conservation grounds alone, we can infer either that they are misinformed about the rate of return or that they intend to be around for some time. We can deduce quite a lot about their time horizons from their investment decisions.

All of this means that the stability of the community in which people live has an important bearing on their perceptions of the future and, in particular, of the future implications of social policy. It is often noted that transient communities generate more serious environmental problems of pollution – litter or vandalism, for example – than stable communities do. This relates directly to the different rates of return on an investment demanded by people living in different communities. In a transient community investments need a quick pay-back period and hence a high rate of return, since time horizons are short. In a stable community a lower rate of return may still seem worth while, given a longer time horizon. A very simple example concerns the matter of tree planting. Obviously, whether a person agrees with paying taxes to have trees planted in her street depends on whether she expects to be around to enjoy them. In a highly transient community no tree can grow fast enough to pay back its sponsors. At the opposite extreme, landed families, who formerly looked forward to dynasties of their offspring living in the same place after them, laid out ambitious estates in the knowledge that these would mature to fruition only after the deaths of the current generation.

Although future utility comes in streams, it is possible to give a present value to an entire stream using a sequence of discount rates, each one relating to a single point in time. This sequence of discount rates is known as a 'discount function'. Time is built into a cost-benefit calculus by calculating the expected utility of an action at each relevant time period, by weighting each pay-off by the appropriate element in the discount function and by then adding these weighted elements into a single 'present value'.

To take a precise example, consider a decision by someone about whether or not to go to university. This is quantified solely in terms of income and income levels over a ten-year period, both for someone who goes and for someone who doesn't go to university, are given in table below. Going to university yields no income for three years (assuming fees and living expenses paid by someone else) and, after that, is expected to yield a steadily rising salary. Not going to university yields an income from the start but one that hits a plateau after five years. The university graduate overtakes the non-graduate in year 6.

CALCULATING A PRESENT VALUE FOR THE FUTURE UTILITY OF A
UNIVERSITY EDUCATION

|  | Go to University | | | Don't Go to University | | |
| --- | --- | --- | --- | --- | --- | --- |
|  | Future | Present value | | Future | Present value | |
|  | income | F1 | F2 | income | F1 | F2 |
|  | (£/year) | (10%) | (5%) | (£/year) | (10%) | (5%) |
| Year 1 | 0 | 0 | 0 | 4,000 | 4,000 | 4,000 |
| Year 2 | 0 | 0 | 0 | 5,000 | 4,500 | 4,750 |
| Year 3 | 0 | 0 | 0 | 6,000 | 4,800 | 5,400 |
| Year 4 | 6,000 | 4,200 | 5,100 | 7,000 | 4,900 | 5,950 |
| Year 5 | 8,000 | 4,800 | 6,400 | 8,000 | 4,800 | 6,400 |
| Year 6 | 10,000 | 5,000 | 7,500 | 8,000 | 4,000 | 6,000 |
| Year 7 | 12,000 | 4,800 | 8,400 | 8,000 | 3,200 | 5,600 |
| Year 8 | 14,000 | 4,200 | 9,100 | 8,000 | 2,400 | 5,200 |
| Year 9 | 16,000 | 3,200 | 9,600 | 8,000 | 1,600 | 4,800 |
| Year 10 | 20,000 | 2,000 | 11,000 | 8,000 | 800 | 4,400 |
| Total present value |  | 28,200 | 57,100 |  | 35,000 | 52,500 |

Imagine two simple discount functions. The first (F1) is such that income is discounted by 10 per cent one year hence, by 20 per cent two years hence, by 60 per cent six years hence and so on. The second (F2) increases at half this rate, so that income is discounted by 5 per cent after one year, 10 per cent after two years, 30 per cent after six years and so on. Thus for a candidate using the first discount function, the present value of a graduate's £10,000 income in year 6 is £5,000. For a candidate using the other discount function it is £7,500.

The total present value of going to university (assuming that no candidate thinks further ahead than ten years) is £28,200 for a candidate using F1 and £57,100 for a candidate using F2. The total present value of *not* going to university, on the other hand, is £35,000 for the first candidate and £52,500 for the second. Thus the first candidate chooses *not* to go, taking a present value of future salaries of £35,000 rather than one of £28,200. The second candidate chooses to go, taking a present value of £57,100 rather than £52,400. The first candidate discounts future salaries more steeply so is *not* prepared to forgo present income for future income. The second discounts future salaries less steeply so *is* prepared to make the short-term investment. Both are perfectly rational but each makes a different decision in the same situation.

Computing the discounted present value of future outcomes may well, of course, be messy in practice. In theory, however, the principle is relatively simple. And this is how we take time into account.

# 5

# Evaluating Outcomes

I have so far ignored the trickiest problem of them all. While looking at the ways in which people evaluate an action by considering its various possible outcomes, I have deferred discussion of the ways in which individuals might put a value on these outcomes in the first place.

There is obviously a very wide range of criteria that people may use to evaluate any particular outcome. If I cook you a meal, you can taste it, smell it, look at it, even eat and digest it. I may produce something that tastes delicious but looks and smells awful, or something that looks wonderful but tastes like silage. There's not much to be gained, in an enterprise such as this, from going into every possible criterion on which any possible outcome might be evaluated. What we can do, however, is to look at some of the very general families of evaluation criteria that share common social properties.

The most obvious set of criteria concerns the personal costs or benefits, to the decision-maker, of any given outcome. We might think of these as direct costs and benefits. While such criteria are clearly important, however, they are certainly not the only ones that people use when they take decisions. Another set concerns the costs and benefits of an outcome to others. Most of us do take the effects of our actions on others into account. The value that is put on these can be thought of as a product of the vicarious cost and benefits of an outcome. A third set of criteria concerns the fact that an outcome opens up options for future actions. If you are a miser, you may enjoy pulling off a huge betting coup simply for the money itself. Unless you get your kicks from rolling around in a bed of crispy banknotes, however, you value money for the options that it opens up for you. You value it for what it will buy rather than for the money itself. Many outcomes have no value in themselves, but are useful only because of the options they generate.

These families of criteria have a different importance for different types of people. Some may be entirely selfish and derive absolutely no pleasure or pain as a result of the effects of their actions on others. Some may be utterly selfless and consider nothing but the effects of their actions on others. Most will consider both families of criteria, though the balance between them may well be one of the things that vary from culture to culture.

## The Direct Costs and Benefits of Consumption

Imagine a sandwich – say, a cheese and pickle sandwich. A sandwich, of course, has many uses, and the value to me of a particular cheese and pickle sandwich will depend upon the uses that I can conceive for it, upon the outcomes that I can imagine. I can squash cockroaches with one or stick it in my ear. I can sit on it or feed it to the dog. I can even eat it.

We can think of each of these uses as giving rise to 'direct consumption' benefits. The satisfactions that I feel from getting rid of cockroaches, from feeding the dog or from filling myself up with cheese and pickle are all things that I consume directly as a result of the sandwich. They are, if you like, what sandwiches are for. *I* consume the good; *I* get the benefit. Furthermore, only I consume the good; only I get the benefit, a matter that is particularly obvious when I eat the sandwich. It ceases, to all intents and purposes, to be a sandwich at all once I have chewed it up and swallowed it.

Thus the most obvious element in any private evaluation of

the outcome concerns the direct private satisfactions for the consumer that arise from that outcome. Few of us forget to include such matters in our decision calculus. Thus, if we consider the outcome of a policy initiative such as the building of a new bridge, we will be sure to note the time and money that we ourselves save on our journeys. We will be sure to notice our own direct costs (measured, for example, in tolls) of using the bridge. And we will be sure to balance the two. Thus when a new (privately funded) bridge over the Liffey was opened in Dublin in 1984, much of the associated publicity concerned the way in which the toll charge to drivers was more than counterbalanced by direct petrol savings to them, in terms of driving miles saved. There are, of course, many other elements in the overall value of a bridge (benefits to non-users from reduced city-centre congestion, for example), but the direct costs and benefits to people who actually drive over the bridge are the most obvious candidates for immediate consideration.

In the same way, a university education may be evaluated in terms of direct salary gains and fee costs to the student; a bus service may be evaluated in terms of time savings and fare costs; and so on. There is little need to dwell on direct costs and benefits to users precisely because they are so evident to those involved. The main point of this chapter is to demonstrate that these are not the *only* factors worthy of consideration in an individual cost-benefit calculus.

## Option Value

One important element in the private evaluation of an outcome yields no direct costs and benefits but is nevertheless a crucial element in its value. This concerns the options that an outcome opens up. People in general value options. They like to 'keep their options open' rather than to 'burn their boats'. Indeed, when a general wantonly destroys his option to retreat, this may frighten opponents precisely because it is such unusual behaviour.

An option to consume future benefits has a real value today – so much so that people are prepared to pay for it. If I expect the price of land to rise, for example, I may well try to buy an option on a building site even though I'm not quite sure whether I will want to build or not. The option may well give me nothing except the right to buy the plot of land in two years' time for £10,000. If the price of building plots in two years' time is £20,000, I will be delighted to exercise the option. If it falls to £5,000 I will not exercise it, as I could easily do better on the open market. Since such an option is giving me something – a right to buy at a fixed price – I must expect to pay for it. Its price will be settled by the balance of supply and demand in much the same way as the price of anything else, though in this case supply and demand will be heavily influenced by different expectations about the future.

Options, therefore, can be traded in the market and have a value in hard cash. There is a highly developed options market in a number of commodities (most notably stocks and shares), and indeed the whole system of dealing in many commodities is often set up to allow people to create effective options for themselves, even if none is formally provided. In practice, however, one of the problems is that only a very limited range of options is available in this way. One of the reasons for this is that most option agreements are rather cumbersome and are not appropriate for many of the goods and services that most people are most interested in.

Consider, for example, the public transport system. Those of us who never use buses none the less benefit from the public bus service in all sorts of ways. Many of these are direct consumption benefits. We benefit from reduced congestion on the roads, from reduced pollution and so on. Our private motoring is, in short, made much more valuable by the existence of public transport. In addition, however, there is the undoubted fact that we could use public transport should we decide to do so.

This option offers further benefits. For example, if I decide to live in a country district that is provided with a regular and reliable bus service, I can run a rather less reliable car than would otherwise be the case in the knowledge that, should my car break down, the bus will always be there to get me to work. My car may never break down, so that I may never exercise my option and consume the bus service, but the option is no less valuable for this. If it did not exist – and it would not exist if the bus service were to be withdrawn – then I would need to run a more reliable car. I would need to pay more money for this, and I would thus find myself faced with real direct costs. If I did not have the extra money, I might be forced to move closer to work and thereby forgo the benefits of country life. The 'option value' of the bus service means that I benefit from it even if I never use it.

Option value has an impact on many aspects of public policy. The health service is an obvious example of something that people like to know is there should they need it, even when they are healthy. In the same way, the education service provides option value to *as yet* childless families and the state housing sector provides option value to families *at present* housed by the private market.

Indeed, as we shall see, housing policy is a very good example of the importance of options. Many are quite happy to be housed where they are now but none the less like to feel that they could move should they want to. They may feel uneasy if changes in the housing system make it more difficult to move house, even if they have no immediate plans to do so. They mourn the loss of their option to move and feel worse off as a result because they cannot now do something that they do not, in fact, currently *want* to do. They feel this way because they can anticipate future circumstances in which they *might* want to move house.

Thus while options are less tangible than many aspects of value, they are actually more straightforward than most, since we are accustomed to paying for future options with cash now.

The problems arise in markets where options are *not* traded and where the option value of a good or service is a crucial component in a decision to support its production. As we shall see, a key problem of public policy concerns relating the raising of costs to the distribution of benefits. In the case of options, this boils down the problem of finding ways to make people to pay for options that they receive from services, even when they do not use these services directly. Thus when I benefit from *your* use of public transport, the problem is how *I* can be made to pay for these benefits, particularly when benefits such as these are a crucial factor in the decision to produce public transport in the first place.

## Vicarious Consumption

The other major element in the private evaluation of any outcome concerns the costs and benefits accruing to *others* as a result of it. Some people are jealous or spiteful. They are made miserable by the good fortune of others and are cheered up by their misery. Other people are altruists whose happiness rises and falls with that of their fellow human beings. Still others are totally indifferent to the well-being of their fellows.

If I contemplate a situation in which you win £1.5 million in a spectacular betting coup and then give none of this to me, I may feel angry and jealous at your good fortune; I may be delighted for you; or I may just shrug my shoulders and stick my nose into yet another pint of Guinness. It all depends on what sort of a person I am and what sort of a mood I'm in. Whatever this is, however, it is likely that *your* private consumption will have some effect on *my* private satisfaction, even when this consumption does not impinge upon me in any direct way. We may call this 'vicarious consumption', the satisfaction or dissatisfaction felt by one person as the direct consequence of consumption by another.

An obvious set of examples concerns the provision of charity. Indeed, the pleasure arising from the giving of any form of gift provides one of the most straightforward forms of vicarious consumption. Of course, people may give gifts in the expectation of receiving something in return, whether it is a favour or merely social approval. (This would apply to someone who gives to charity in a public bar collection, not because of a basic desire to help others but either because she does not want to seem the odd one out or because she wants to impress others who might be watching.) Many gifts, however, are given for the pleasure of providing enjoyment to others. In such cases, the greater the pleasure to others, the greater the vicarious satisfaction arising from the gift. We have all felt the effects of this phenomenon while choosing a present for someone or while eagerly watching the recipient's face as the present is unwrapped.

In more general terms, we nearly all accept the need to contribute towards social welfare provisions for the needy because the suffering of others, for one reason or another, makes us feel uncomfortable. We vicariously consume welfare benefits that help others.

The distinction between direct and vicarious consumption is not clear-cut, particularly when we are dealing with individuals who are closely related to one another. Within a family, for example, it may be difficult to decide whether the things that parents often want for their children (a good education, say, or a 'suitable' marriage partner) are really wanted vicariously for the children or selfishly for the parents. This particular problem is usually resolved by taking the household rather than the individual as the fundamental unit of analysis. Even so, the distinction between direct and vicarious consumption can be a hard one to make. Given the fact that many ethical codes rank the helping of others as a worthier activity than helping yourself, the scope for self-delusion is obviously considerable.

Notwithstanding this, we will obviously miss out on a crucial element in a person's evaluation of an outcome if we consider only direct benefits to the decision-maker. People *do* give blood freely; they *do* make donations to charity; and they *do* accept the making of tax payments that are distributed as welfare provisions for the needy. And they can't all be deluding themselves or bowing to social pressure.

Direct private consumption and indirect vicarious consumption thus comprise two broad categories within a particular outcome that may be evaluated by an individual. Direct and vicarious evaluations may operate in the same direction, or they may operate in opposite directions. Most gifts, for example, reduce the resources available to the giver for her private consumption, costing money, time and/or effort. To offset these losses, the gift provides vicarious satisfaction if it is enjoyed by the recipient. Other outcomes yield both private and vicarious benefits. Many students value a good degree, for example, both because they want one for themselves and because they are made happy by the pleasure that the good degree provides for their parents. (In the same way, those very parents are happy both because of their private pride in their offspring and because the degree may help their children towards a better life.) The obvious problem, therefore, is how to combine direct and vicarious costs and benefits into one single evaluation of any given outcome.

## Combining Direct and Vicarious Aspects of Value

We have already seen that the various criteria used to evaluate an action must be capable of being reduced to a single common denominator if a decision is to be made. While a cost-benefit calculus can be performed in a number of different currencies, which might well include direct and vicarious utility, there is ultimately a need to trade off one criterion against another. This involves specifying quite how much vicarious satisfaction balances how much direct personal cost, for example, or quite what level of selfish gain is an acceptable trade-off against a certain level of vicarious loss.

Most of us are prepared to pay a penny to save a life of a total stranger, while few would be prepared to sacrifice their entire family for the life of the same person. We all draw the line somewhere, and precisely where we draw the line is determined by the rate at which we trade off direct costs and benefits against those that are vicarious. Many of us don't like to admit that we do this. When we draw the line, after all, we are stating that we will help others no more than we have helped them already.

The factors that determine *where* we draw the line can be very complex. Most people, for example, derive greater vicarious pleasure from helping people they know than from helping people they don't know. The mass media can have a great impact on this process. Consider the recent and interesting social phenomenon of the 'disaster fund' that can generate huge sums in charitable donations for the families of accident victims or for children who need expensive surgery. The success of such funds depends crucially upon the personalities of the recipients being established firmly by the media in the minds of potential donors. The donors who contribute to such a fund have often ignored many appeals to help equally needy people, presumably because the recipients have been presented anonymously as one of a mass of 'starving children', 'cancer victims' or whatever. When people don't know *precisely* who the recipients of charitable donations are, they seem none the less more likely to give when they have some point of personal identification. Thus the sudden upsurge of donations to help Ethiopian famine victims in November 1984 was related very specifically to the broadcasting of horrifying news film, including close-up shots of children actually starving to death. Film close-ups obviously personalize matters much more effectively than, for example, newspaper reports. Newspapers had, in fact, been reporting the horrors of the Ethiopian famine for some time before the TV cameras. It was the TV close-ups, however, that elicited the mass charitable response.

While it may seem hard-hearted to say this, the fact remains that most people do trade off personal pleasure against vicarious satisfaction. Many give generously to charity, of course, but rather few give so generously that they place themselves in serious financial difficulties. Thus while we may not like to admit that we draw a line, and while we may draw it rather inconsistently depending on all kinds of circumstances, we all draw one none the less. We trade off direct and vicarious consumption and reach a point where we will help others no more.

It is useful for most purposes to think of this process as the straightforward application of some form of exchange rate. This has the advantage of providing an evaluation of any outcome in a single currency to facilitate the type of cost-benefit calculus that I have already described.

An alternative method is to conduct a separate cost-benefit calculus for each currency in which the outcomes are denominated. We might, for example, select the best outcome on vicarious grounds, the best one on selfish grounds and so on. When the same action is selected, regardless of the currency used, there is no problem. When different cost-benefit analyses identify different actions, then a means is needed of deciding between them. One method of doing this is to use the criteria in a strict and predetermined order. If the first criterion in the ordering unequivocally identifies an action as the optimum, then that action is selected. If not, a *set* of actions must have been identified as equally desirable in terms of the first criterion. The second criterion is then applied to this set. Subsequent criteria are applied in this way until a unique action is selected. Thus the first criterion totally dominates all others. The second dominates all criteria but the first and so on. This is known as a 'lexicographic' ordering of criteria.

Three actions, for example, might be evaluated as follows on the basis of criteria of direct and of vicarious satisfaction:

|  | DIRECT SATISFACTION | VICARIOUS SATISFACTION |
|---|---|---|
| Action 1 | $X$ units | $10Y$ units |
| Action 2 | $2X$ units | $Y$ units |
| Action 3 | $X$ units | $Y$ units |

We can see straightaway that action 3 is *dominated* by the other two. There is no reason to select it rather than action 1, which yields the same direct satisfaction as action 3 and ten times as much vicarious satisfaction. Neither is there any reason to select action 3 rather than action 2, which yields the same vicarious satisfaction but twice as much direct satisfaction. The two criteria produce conflicting evaluations of the relative merits of action 1 and 2, however. If vicarious satisfaction is used on its own, then action 1 is selected. If only direct satisfaction is considered, then action 2 is selected.

We may, as we have seen, trade off the two criteria and make a decision. We may decide that direct and vicarious satisfaction should be weighted equally and then choose action 1, which yields eleven 'units' of satisfaction as opposed to the three units yielded by action 2. Or we may decide that direct satisfaction is twenty times more important than vicarious satisfaction, in which case we will select action 2.

When we order the criteria lexicographically, however, we are in effect stating that no amount of added value on the second criterion compensates for any loss, however small, measured in terms of the first. If we ranked the criterion of direct satisfaction above that of vicarious satisfaction, we would then unequivocally select action 2. If we ranked the criteria in the reverse order, we would unequivocally select action 1. Even if the direct satisfaction of action 2 were to increase a thousandfold, it would not change our decision, since no loss of vicarious satisfaction could compensate for this. This does not, however, amount to ignoring direct satisfaction entirely. Action 2, for example, is preferred to action 3 because of its higher direct benefits, despite the equal rating of the two actions in terms of vicarious satisfaction.

A lexicographic ordering of criteria would thus be the technique used by a selfish, yet sociable, person who felt prepared to help others, provided only that this did not harm her one little bit. Alternatively, we might find an altogether more saintly sort of person who would do things to benefit herself only provided that no one else was harmed at all. In either case, the key point is that the separate criteria of value are never combined into a single evaluation but are kept quite distinct.

Any number of sets of criteria can be ranked in this way, just as any number can be traded off against one another – though the process can obviously get extremely complex. In general terms, however, in the pages that follow we will be working for the most part with two criteria, the direct and the vicarious costs and benefits of an outcome, though option value will also be used to provide an added dimension to each of these.

To conclude, the two general families of evaluation criteria that I shall be using relate to the direct consumption of costs and benefits by the person making the evaluation and to her vicarious interest in the consumption of others. Between the two of them these two families of criteria cover most of the ways in which most people are likely to evaluate outcomes, though the way in which direct and vicarious consumption are traded off against one another will obviously vary dramatically between individuals and may also vary systematically between cultures.

# 6

# Spillovers and Public Goods: the Effects of Actions on Others

So far we have looked only at the evaluation of actions by the actor herself. While we have included vicarious satisfactions in this calculus, these are nevertheless benefits that accrue to the person who takes the decision. We have thus far ignored the costs and benefits that actions visit upon others, a matter that we must clearly take into account before we can analyse the *social* costs and benefits of any action.

Imagine, for example, that I give you a brand-new motorbike for your birthday. You will no doubt be delighted. I will derive great vicarious satisfaction from your delight.

Your parents, however, may well plumb the very depths of misery at the thought of you roaring all over town on a brand-new Kawasaki. The health service, meanwhile, must brace itself for another accident victim. The Minister for Finance will sigh wearily at yet another blow to the balance of payments figures. In short, my simple gift to you of a few hundredweight of throbbing metal generates a whole constellation of costs and benefits to others. These are the 'spillovers' of my action in giving you the bike. In general we can think of spillovers as the costs and benefits generated for other people as a result of decisions taken by any given actor. Some of these spillovers may be beneficial. (You, at least, are delighted to consume the spillover effects of my vicarious pleasure in giving away motorbikes.) Some may be harmful. (The same act induces great misery in your parents.) Either way, the effect of spillovers on others may well be profound.

There are a number of aspects to the production of spillovers that influence the implications that they have for policy-makers. In the first place, they may be *intentional* or *unintentional*. Very often, of course, spillovers are unintentional. I did not, after all, set out to make your parents miserable when I bought you the motorbike, just as I do not set out to pollute the environment when I go driving in my car. The fact that spillovers are often unintended, however, is of little consequence to those who are forced to suffer them.

In practice, many of the major spillovers with which we shall be concerned are produced as unintended side-effects of actions motivated by quite different reasons. Just as the beneficial public spillovers of art or innovation are produced almost as by-products of the private creative activity of artists or inventors, the damaging public spillovers of pollution are typically by-products of private individuals who do not mean any harm.

Indeed, it is useful to think of pollution as a generic example of unintended damaging spillovers. The emissions from a factory chimney represent the classic case, since they are a method for broadcasting the waste products of a particular production process over the surrounding area. The production process is generally engaged in for private profit. The waste products *can* be treated at source to reduce their damaging effects, though often at a cost that significantly reduces the private profitability of the operation. Nevertheless the cost of treating the waste products at source is typically much less than the total cost of repairing the damage that they do once they have escaped into the environment. Thus the social costs of pollution often outweigh the private gains to the polluter. While this last factor is not a necessary condition for pollution to represent a policy problem, it defines a situation in which it would even be cost-effective for the victims of pollution to pay the polluter to treat her own waste products at source.

In pollution, therefore, we have a standard example of an activity that is an *unintended*, though often a *known*, consequence of the utility-maximizing activities of a particular actor.

While the actor does not choose to cause the pollution, she does choose not to treat the pollution caused as a side-effect of her activity. While, traditionally, pollution has been thought of in terms of the chemical waste products of domestic or commercial activity (including smoke, sewage, noxious gases, spent radioactive fuels and so on), it does make sense to think of it in much broader terms. People now talk of noise pollution from aircraft and even from ghetto-blaster hifi units. We might also, however, think in terms of architectural pollution from ugly commercial property developments, of environmental pollution from the clearing of forests or the destruction of other natural amenities, of animal pollution from the urban rampages of poorly controlled domestic pets and so on. In each case we are referring to situations in which others pay some of the costs of an action that yields a 'profit' for the person who is making the decisions.

As we shall see in chapter 10, pollution problems represent one of the most clear-cut justifications for regulatory action by government, usually designed to force polluters to pay a higher share of the social costs of their actions by forcing them to take steps either to prevent, or to mop up, the spillovers they cause.

In contrast to spillovers that take the form of pollution, there is a class of *beneficial* side-effects of private utility-maximizing activity. Most scientific discoveries, for example, provide benefits for society as a whole as a result of the 'selfish' research programmes of scientists. The profound social consequences of the radio, the car, the car radio and the non-stick frying pan are the results of the efforts of people who did not set out to change the world but who succeeded in doing so none the less. Indeed, it is almost axiomatic that the social consequences of most scientific discoveries cannot be accurately foreseen. Certainly, many technological 'break-throughs' that have threatened to change our lives have turned out to be damp squibs, while the real changes have often come from unexpected directions.

Some spillovers, however, are intentional, and there is a class of intentional spillovers that are valued almost entirely for their public effects. We all enjoy the good that is produced when private individuals take certain precautions relating to basic personal hygiene, such as washing their hands before preparing our food. There are some personal benefits to the hand-washer in such a precaution, but by far and away its greatest value is as a public health measure. While enhanced public health is a spillover of such private actions, it is a spillover that is much more important than the direct benefits to the original actors. In such circumstances people often do set out to generate spillovers, and the spillovers that are so generated are usually called 'public goods'.

A public good, therefore, is a special class of spillover effect, in which the consequences of the spillover simply swamp those of the individual action. Public goods present serious policy problems for precisely this reason, since the private benefits to each decision-maker that arise *as a direct consequence* of a decision to contribute to producing the good typically do not merit the costs. This is usually because a public good can be consumed by people *regardless of whether they contribute to it*. This gives people very little private incentive to contribute and hence causes the good to be seriously under-produced. The problem of producing public goods, or beneficial spillovers, is thus a form of collective-action problem.

The classic example of a public good is a lighthouse. On the shores of Lough Corrib in County Galway there is a (ruined) private lighthouse, constructed for a private company that made extensive commercial use of the lake. This, however, is very much the exception. Typically, those who erect lighthouses may also consume their benefits, but many others may do so also, regardless of whether they have paid a penny towards the costs of building or maintaining the light. The light spills out over the sea, visible to all sailors, and is a very pure version of a public good. For this reason it is difficult to see how a lighthouse could be run as a money-making venture; despite its obvious social benefits, it is unlikely to be produced by the private market. Whether we regard the lighthouse as a public good or as a spillover does not really matter. The key point is that the private costs and benefits are insufficient to motivate certain actions with highly valued social spillover effects. When almost nothing but the spillovers is significant, the outcome tends in practice to be called a public good.

The second important social property of a spillover is that it may be either *optional* or *compulsory*. When I light a cigar, for example, you suffer the spillover effects of my smoke. But you may leave the room if you wish, or at least give me a wide berth. You can choose to opt out of paying some of the cost of my pleasure, though only at a certain inconvenience. If I, as an artist, produce another new masterpiece, it costs nothing for you, a philistine, to ignore it completely. On the other hand, when I start the serious testing of a new form of nuclear missile, you can escape the spillover effects of my actions only by emigrating to another planet. My masterpiece is optional, but my missile is compulsory. My cigar smoke is neither; it is *relatively* optional, in the sense that in order to avoid it you must incur some personal cost.

Considering the effects of noise pollution from an airport, it is clear that the sound of a jumbo jet taking off is not a matter that can easily be ignored by nearby residents. A large aircraft at close quarters generates a range of compulsory spillovers, and a noise meter even offers the prospect of quantifying some of these in terms of decibels. A person living some distance away from the airport may suffer some inconvenience in summer, when flights are more frequent and the warmer weather makes spending time in the garden more attractive. Further away still, the aircraft noise may affect only those who own recording studios and who must pay a little more for sound insulation if they don't want their recordings ruined once in a while. In short, the same noise pollution has a degree of 'optionality' in almost direct proportion to a person's distance from the source. It can be quantified rather precisely as the cost that an individual must engage in to exclude herself from the spillover. Thus a person living near the end of the main runway at Heathrow airport might need to spend several thousands of pounds in order to soundproof an average private house, while a person living 50 miles away might need only to close a window on a couple of days a year.

A matter related to whether a spillover is optional or not concerns whether it is *indiscriminate* or can be *targeted*. Some spillovers can be channelled in certain directions, but others cannot. A classic example of an indiscriminate spillover is commercial broadcast television. The actual programmes that are transmitted by commercial television companies are side-effects of the main business that they are conducting, which is the selling of an audience to advertisers. The revenue for commercial TV comes from advertisers, not viewers, and advertisers are buying a certain audience, not the programmes. The entire programme content of a commercial TV station is thus a spillover, and, once it is broadcast on the airwaves, it is also indiscriminate. Anyone within range and with a TV receiver can watch the programmes. No one can be prevented from doing so, save by being locked up.

Despite all of this, of course, the fact that TV or radio broadcasts are indiscriminate does not mean that they are in any sense compulsory. It costs nothing to leave the TV turned off, and for this reason broadcasting provides a very good generic example of the indiscriminate spillover.

A good example of a spillover that can be targeted can be found in the heat emissions of a power station. Such emissions are an inevitable consequence of the generation of electricity, but they can be broadcast into the atmosphere (and effectively thrown away) or channelled to those who might value them. Thus some power stations now sell their spillover heat to local market gardeners for use in their greenhouses.

The distinction between targeted and indiscriminate spillovers is particularly important for those that are evaluated in *positive* fashion. It is unlikely that the producers of negative spillovers will vindictively target these at certain victims. Where positive spillovers are involved, however, the possibility of targeting these has a significant impact on their funding. When spillovers can be targeted, and hence sold, funding can be raised on a 'pay-as-you-use' principle that can never be employed for those that are indiscriminate. The enormous difficulties associated with raising revenue from TV users is a case in point, and virtually all indiscriminate positive spillovers must be funded on the basis of general taxation if they are to be funded at all.

From this it can be seen that the problem of producing public goods depends crucially on whether or not the good concerned is indiscriminate. Indeed, while all goods are to a greater or lesser extent public goods in the sense that they have public consequences, and while many goods may be such that their public consequences swamp their private costs and benefits, those that are also indiscriminate are the ones that generate the most acute problems of production and can be thought of as 'pure' public goods.

Thus a lighthouse is a pure public good, since it is indiscriminate in its effect. A satellite navigation system based on coded radio frequencies is not indiscriminate in the sense that the codes can be released only to certain people. The system can be targeted and thereby financed by user charges.

However, the existence of such a targeted system still has enormous public consequences. Planes thus navigated do not land on my head; I and my loved ones survive long journeys; the world in general is transformed by the improvement in its transportation systems. If people do not use such navigation systems, few will argue that this is a matter for their purely private decision. When an airplane not using the navigation system crashes in the middle of a densely populated area, the owner no doubt feels very sorry that she tried to save a little money. But it is clear that the spillover effects of her action swamp any private cost-benefit calculus that she might have conducted.

The point of this example is to demonstrate that there is a class of goods and services that have the property that they can be targeted but are such that the spillover effects none the less swamp the private cost-benefit calculus. Because they may be bought and sold, they are not *pure* public goods. But because of their overwhelmingly important spillovers, they are *very* public goods nevertheless. The generic example here is public liability insurance.

People engaged in dangerous pursuits, such as driving, are often obliged by law to hold public liability insurance. Because such insurance can be targeted to policy-holders, it can be bought and sold and, indeed, is normally supplied in this way by the market. Because a person can cause much more damage with her car, for example, than she could ever conceivably repay in a full working lifetime, the magnitude of the potential spillovers caused by drivers are such that a policy of enforcing universal public liability insurance for all drivers can be held to be a desirable public good. As the potential innocent accident victims of bankrupt drivers, all gain from the policy.

The fact that such insurance can be, and usually is, targeted does not mean, given its immense spillover benefits, that it must necessarily be produced in this way. An alternative would be for the state to fund an insurance system out of a special tax levy on petrol, for example. Such a policy would have a number of attractive features. Payments would be proportional to the petrol consumed and hence to the amount of driving engaged in. It would not be possible to drive while uninsured, and there would thus also be a considerable saving in enforcement costs. To be set against this is the fact that potentially dangerous drivers would pay the same premiums as safe ones and that some separate methods of penalizing dangerous driving would need to be implemented. (It is currently the case that insurance loadings constitute a more severe financial penalty than most fines for motoring offences. Certainly, drunken drivers tend to be punished much more severely by private insurance companies than by the courts.) The key point illustrated by the generic example of public liability insurance, however, is that there are at the very least two independent aspects of the 'publicness' of a good. On the one hand, indiscriminate goods are 'more public' than others because they are available to all if they are available at all. On the other hand, very specifically targeted goods, such as public liability insurance, may be such that their spillover effects swamp any private costs and benefits.

A further important social property of spillovers concerns their remoteness from the action that generates them. All spillovers are indirect, but some are more indirect than others. When I give you a Kawasaki, a very direct spillover is the misery of your parents. An equally direct effect is a decline in the health of the nation's balance of payments account. Flowing from this, the exchange rate is affected. As a consequence of this, the cost of imported salami increases, and fewer people buy it. This may lead to lay-offs in Italian salami factories, and unemployed salami workers will have less to spend in their local shops. . . . And so on.

In this sense, each action that we take is rather like dropping a pebble into an infinitely large pool. Ripples spread out around the splash, and they continue for ever. Precisely how far away from the splash we should look before we are satisfied that we have looked at the *total* outcome of the action, however, is a matter of opinion rather than of fact. Some people will take a relatively broad view, being prepared to consider small ripples at great distances from the original splash. Others will not. A line has to be drawn somewhere, and where it is in fact drawn is another matter that tends to vary between different policy systems.

Take the policy area of land-use planning control, for example. Building development is a very good example of something that provides direct private *benefits* to the individuals who do the development and indirect spillover *costs* to others. When I erect an ugly house in the middle of a beautiful landscape, on land that is indisputably owned by me, public perceptions of the spillover effects of this action may vary from culture to culture. One of the costs of my private pleasure is that the landscape is spoiled for others. (When I am in the house looking out at what is left of the beautiful landscape, it doesn't seem spoiled to me.)

There is a clear tendency for people in certain cultural environments to discount the more indirect spillover costs of such building development. When a person builds a house on a piece of private land, it is seen much more as her own private business in some places than it would be elsewhere. The level of planning control in parts of the United States, for example, is much less rigorous than it is in the centres of many historic Italian cities, where, by contrast, almost any change to a person's house or land can affect the overall character of the street or neighbourhood. People seem much more willing to accept very strict controls over such changes because the public consequences of this are perceived much more acutely. Considering the number of private property developers over the centuries who must have coveted sites in downtown Venice or Florence, for example, it is remarkable that the land-use planning systems in these cities have been able to resist the pressure. There must be a much greater willingness to consider broader conceptions of the 'publicness' of a 'private' building in these cities than can be found elsewhere. Even repainting the window frames of your house a different colour, for example, may spoil the look of a beautiful terrace. In certain parts of Europe people are apparently prepared to consider such a terrace to be the 'property' not just of the owner, not even just of those who live in the city, but of all those who have some sort of an interest in the general cultural heritage that the city represents.

To summarize, we have explored a number of social properties that we may use to classify spillovers. Each of these has an implication for the likely implications of a given spillover for public policy. Thus spillovers may be:

> positive or negative
> more, or less, optional
> more, or less, indiscriminate
> more, or less, direct.

The social implications of each of these independent properties can be characterized by a set of generic examples that symbolize the main issues at stake. Thus pollution is a generic example of a negative spillover, TV or radio broadcasting a generic example of an indiscriminate spillover, public liability insurance a generic example of a targeted spillover and so on.

In previous chapters we considered the distinctions between 'selfish' and 'vicarious' evaluations of the effects of an action, and between the actual consumption of these effects and the existence of options to consume them. Both vicarious evaluations and option values can apply to the spillovers of actions as well as to the actions themselves. Thus if you close off access to a particular beach by fencing your private land, for example, my option to use the beach is eliminated. I may never have used the beach, nor may I plan to, but I may nevertheless feel worse off as a result of your action. A spillover of it is to close off my options. I may even feel vicariously sorry for someone else whose options are closed off in this way, particularly while viewing a heartrending TV documentary about a bunch of previously happy children made miserable by your selfish act. And I may want something done about the problem.

We may summarize the various dimensions of value that we have so far considered in the chart below.

|  | SELFISH EVALUATION | | VICARIOUS EVALUATION | |
|  | *Consumer-controlled actions* | *Spillover effects* | *Consumer-controlled actions* | *Spillover effects* |
| --- | --- | --- | --- | --- |
| Actual consumption value | A | B | E | F |
| Option value | C | D | G | H |

Most of us will feel most familiar with the aspect of value defined by category A, that which is selfishly appreciated, actually consumed and consumer-controlled. This, of course, is the aspect of value that the market as we know it tends to deal in. In the realm of mass transportation, therefore, the market can deal in the buying and selling of private cars or the profitable operation of private bus companies and airlines. Such markets involve the selling of actual transportation benefits to the selfish consumer and tend, as far as possible, to ignore the spillover effects of this activity. The most intangible aspect of value can be found in category H, defining that which is vicarious, optional and beyond the control of the actor concerned. Yet, even within the realm of mass transportation, I *may* be concerned to let others have the opportuity to live near city-centre streets unclogged by private cars. My concern would *vicariously* involve the *option* value to others of a positive *spillover* from the operation of a public transport system. But it might be a concern none the less.

# 7

# The Social Evaluation of Actions

We have just seen that an individual decision-maker will evaluate an outcome on the basis of her 'selfish' direct consumption costs and benefits, of the costs and benefits arising from her vicarious evaluation of the consumption of others and of the costs and benefits of the *options* that her actions generate. When we consider only a single individual, we have seen that, despite the fact that she may use many denominators of value, she will ultimately take a decision that will reflect the way in which these different denominators interact with one another. Whether or not people actually do make trade-offs in this way, we may proceed as if they do and interpret their decisions accordingly.

We have also seen that virtually all actions have spillover effects on others. These are consequences of an action for individuals other than the actor. Individual actions, therefore, will typically be evaluated by quite a wide range of people. This means that the next task is to find a way to combine the various evaluations of a particular action made by non-actors in order to produce an estimate of its net 'social' effect.

When we wish to describe how groups of individuals evaluate outcomes, we face a very serious problem. This concerns the *theoretical impossibility*, despite the *practical necessity*, of comparing the value attached by two or more people to the same thing.

Imagine a situation in which you and I are squabbling over a new toy – let's say an expensive portable word-processor. We each want to take it home for the night. Each of us, of course, feels that our own need is far greater than the other's. I may make a long speech about how great my need is, strutting up and down, shouting, even banging the table with my fist. When it's your turn, you do the same, attempting to shout louder and bang harder than I have. When we have both subsided we will be no closer to finding out who most needs the word-processor than we were at the beginning. Even King Solomon would face a hard job in deciding which of us felt most strongly about the matter. How can we compare what I feel with what you feel? When I say that I *really* want the word-processor, and you say that you *really, really, really* want it, where does that leave us? Once I want the contraption even a little bit, why don't I have every incentive to exaggerate my feelings in order to get it? Yet, if we never compare the evaluations made by different individuals, how can we ever make a social decision? In short, when we wish to compare evaluations made by two different people, we must compare their *feelings* about the world. In principle, of course, this is impossible. In practice, however, one of the things that policy-makers simply must do is to make some estimate of the *social* impact of actions. The basic problem is that this involves adding the evaluations of different individuals. Because these cannot, in principle, be compared with one another, they cannot be added together. If we cannot aggregate several individual evaluations into a single collective evaluation, we cannot compare the social impact of alternative actions or policies. In practice, of course, we do this all the time. And we do so by adopting one or other highly imperfect solution to the problem of comparing individual evaluations.

Another matter that we need to settle concerns whether or not it makes sense to talk about the value of an outcome to the *group as a whole* as opposed to its combined value to *each group member*. I have so far taken a very individualistic line by assuming that the value of an outcome is recorded and appreciated by individual decision-makers rather than by a group as a whole. To do otherwise creates very tricky problems, but a more collective view may none the less be more appropriate.

In order to give a practical effect to the more collective view, we must specify what we mean when we say that something is valuable for a group, yet not for its individual members. Does it make sense, for example, to say that 'farmers' will benefit from a particular policy, even when no individual farmer benefits? In certain circumstances it may indeed seem reasonable to make statements such as this. We all know, for example, that a riot is much, much more than a thousand people simply behaving as individuals. There is something about putting those people together into a riot that adds a new dimension to the decisions they make. Many sports fans relish the atmosphere of a live match, and make great sacrifices to attend, when they could get a much better view of the sporting action by sitting at home and watching television. Sometimes, as we know, the atmosphere of a live match can even provoke a riot. Yet does a group such as this actually have a *collective mind*, or is what makes its decisions special simply a product of the very complex interactions between individuals that take place in certain highly charged social situations?

My contention will be that an evaluation made by a group is ultimately no more than the aggregated evaluations of its members. This argument only holds water, however, once we have taken into account the full consequences of the vicarious consumption and spillover effects to which I have already referred. I will begin by discussing this problem and will return later to the matter of how to produce a group evaluation of a given outcome by adding together the evaluations of the individual members.

## On the Collective Whole and its Individual Parts

Consider something that we might, on the face of it, wish to argue is good for a group but bad for its members. Consider conformity.

It is sometimes argued that a group 'wants' or 'needs' members to conform to certain norms of behaviour, even when the members themselves do not want to do so. It is certainly true that the pressures to conform to group norms can often seem very intense and that these pressures appear to be felt by the individual to come from the group. It may well be the case that *no* member wants to conform to the norms of a particular group and yet that *all* do conform because *each* values the benefits of group membership.

The problem is not to explain why people conform. Conformity is perfectly rational for those who face real or imagined group sanctions and who want to remain part of the group. The problem is to explain why the group 'wants' its members to conform. When we say that the group values conformity even when the members do not, we may be adopting one of two basic approaches.

In the first place, we may be viewing the group *from the outside*. In doing so, we may feel that we can take a more enlightened or comprehensive view of the welfare of the individual members than they themselves are capable of appreciating. If we do this, we are, in effect, constructing an argument either about false consciousness or about spillovers.

We might, for example, be saying that, while people don't think that they value conformity, they would value it if only they could see their 'real' interests. Alternatively we might be saying that, if people don't conform, the social consequences for the group may be damaging. (If one of the norms is honesty, for example, then each might quite rationally be dishonest, but the consequent social chaos would damage all.) Either way, we would be asserting that the difference between the value of something to the group and the aggregate value to the members arises from their mistaken perceptions of value. We might even assert that group members will *inevitably* be mistaken about this but would still be doing no more than imposing what we see as a superior individualistic calculus. We would still be assuming that group benefits are consumed by individuals, albeit in ways that they cannot themselves foresee or even appreciate. We would be claiming to be more enlightened than group members, but this would not amount to an assertion that the group had a distinctive collective mind.

Notwithstanding this, we may well refer to the collection of members as a 'group', and the members themselves may well think of the group as a distinctive entity. Indeed, it *is* a group for most practical purposes. When we refer to what the group 'wants', however, we are still referring to what its *members* want.

This approach reflects a tradition of public policy-making going back to Plato and no doubt even earlier. Part of the essence of Plato's theory of public policy was to isolate policy-makers from the groups that they administered, precisely so that they would be able to take a more 'objective', or at least a more disinterested, view of group welfare. Ever since then policy-makers have rarely been short of ideas about what groups of (other) people *really* want. Whether we see this as an elitist or as a visionary approach usually depends upon whether we agree with the specific ideas involved. The key point that remains, however, is that the fact that outside observers can see a group as a single, even an organic, entity does not meant that the group itself has a will over and above the wills of its members.

Rather than viewing the group 'from the outside', we may nevertheless argue that there are *intrinsic* benefits in group conformity that can be perceived, despite the fact that they are not valued, by group members. Here we may be talking about the essentially social outcomes of group activity, like group solidarity or *esprit de corps*, that make no sense at all when considered in terms of isolated individuals.

These social outcomes are most important, of course, but they are still appreciated by individuals, whether these are outside observers or group members. Thus, while we might want to say that the 'group' has gained something at the expense of its members, and while the members of the group might even agree, we would all still be talking about our respective individual evaluations of the situation. Such evaluations might well be vicarious and not at all 'selfish' in the sense that people get no *direct* benefits from the solidarity of the group in question, but this does not matter. What it goes to show is that the entities from which people can derive vicarious satisfaction do not necessarily need to be individuals.

The fact that we can get vicarious pleasure from the consumption, for example, of 'future generations', 'the poor', 'children' or whoever else does not mean that the fundamental accounting unit is not the individual. Vicarious consumption, of course, does vastly broaden the scope of cost-benefit analysis. But it is the *vicariousness* of some of the major sources of utility for an individual that is important, not the fact that people may be vicariously affected by the fate of social groups rather than by that of individuals.

This is a very important point. We should not confuse the fact that we often find it useful to perceive a group as some form of corporate entity with the possibility that the same group has some form of corporate mind.

I hope that all of this is not mere playing with words. It is an attempt to show that there is more than one way of moving beyond an narrowly individualistic, and obviously unsatisfactory, method of evaluating social outcomes. The understandable desire to impute a collective value to outcomes can be satisfied in two obvious ways. One is to develop some notion of a collective mind, and I have tried to show that this is difficult to get to grips with. The other is to rely upon the notion of vicarious consumption, together with the idea that people have a vicarious interest in the fate of collectivities as well as that of individuals. In this case the vicarious consumer is still an individual.

Thus I may feel happy if the lot of 'the poor' is improved by a new welfare measure. It is still I, an individual, who feel happy, however, while each *individual* member of 'the poor' feels happy if her lot is improved. If someone decides to 'improve' the lot of the poor by removing their social welfare benefits (allowing them to enjoy the camaraderie of collective poverty, for example, and to develop their individual and collective self-reliance), that person may derive *individual* vicarious satisfaction from the act. If every poor person is thereby made to feel worse off, however, it is difficult to see how the statement that, notwithstanding this, 'the poor are now collectively better off' is anything more than an individual opinion.

This latter approach seems to me to raise far fewer problems, while still achieving all that we might want. In the same way that we can derive satisfaction from the existence of a healthy tree without needing to feel that the tree itself is enjoying its good health, we can derive satisfaction from some wider notion of group well-being without needing to assume that the group has a collective mind.

## Adding the Individual Parts into a Collective Whole

When we looked at the problem facing an individual who evaluates an action on the basis of a range of incompatible criteria, we saw one circumstance in which the problem disappeared. This was when all criteria selected the same action as the most valuable. We had you working for a good degree, you'll remember, both because you wanted one for yourself and because you derived vicarious pleasure from satisfying your parents.

In much the same way, even though we cannot strictly combine the evaluations of two or more separate individuals, there may be situations in which *all* individuals prefer one particular outcome to the others. There may be other situations in which *some* people *prefer* one particular outcome to an alternative, while *all of the others* are quite *indifferent* to either. We can still say that the first outcome is socially preferred, and few would disagree. Nobody rates it lower than the alternative, and some rate it higher. In such circumstances we do have a quite uncontroversial principle for making a social evaluation. The principle involved is known as the Pareto Principle.

Unfortunately, such circumstances are not very common. When some members of a group rate one outcome higher while others rate an alternative higher, the Pareto Principle will not help us decide. We must then weigh the evaluations of some against the evaluations of others, using some form of Utility Principle.

## The Pareto Principle

The Pareto Principle selects A over B if, and only if, at least one prefers A to B and none prefers B to A (in other words, if all who do not positively prefer A are indifferent between A and B). The great advantage of the Pareto Principle is that it enables us to combine individual into social evaluations while making as few value judgements as possible. We need to know only that three people rate option A over option B, for example, to know that all three, 'collectively', prefer A. We need make no assumptions about either the extent or the nature of the individual preferences concerned.

For those situations in which there *is* a single outcome that dominates all others for all individuals in the group, there can, of course, be little argument with the Pareto Principle. The problem is that such situations are extremely rare. Obviously, the bigger the group, the more rarely such situations occur.

If we turn the Pareto Principle into a voting system, for example, we will ignore abstentions but then demand unanimous approval by all who vote. Other things being equal, the more people who vote, the less we can expect absolute unanimity. We might not, for example, be surprised to find three or four people in unanimous agreement about something. We would be astonished to find no dissenting voice in 3 million or 4 million. Yet one dissenting voice confounds the Pareto Principle, and we cannot then use it to make social decisions. (This is because, strictly, we cannot say that the one person made worse off is not damaged so much that the gains of a million others will not compensate for this.)

This is compounded by the fact that attempting to use the Pareto Principle in situations where there is not one dominant outcome can result either in a total inability to make decisions or in decisions that can be perverse and often extremely conservative.

Consider the chart below, which gives rankings of three outcomes by ten people. The chart lists only the *order* in which each of the ten people (A to J) rank outcomes 1, 2 and 3. Note that no interpersonal comparisons of utility are needed to derive this information, which depends only on the personal evaluation of the options by each individual.

|           | A   | B   | C   | D   | E   | F   | G   | H   | I   | J   |
|-----------|-----|-----|-----|-----|-----|-----|-----|-----|-----|-----|
| Outcome 1 | 1st | 1st | 1st | 1st | 1st | 1st | 1st | 1st | 1st | 2nd |
| Outcome 2 | 2nd | 2nd | 2nd | 2nd | 2nd | 2nd | 2nd | 2nd | 2nd | 1st |
| Outcome 3 | 3rd | 3rd | 3rd | 3rd | 3rd | 3rd | 3rd | 3rd | 3rd | 3rd |

Forget about outcome 1 for a minute and look only at outcomes 2 and 3. The group may discover a large oilfield, for example, worth £1 million a year, and may be trying to decide how to divide the profits. If the well had been dry they would each have had nothing – this is outcome 3. After the gusher they must share the £1 million. One possibility is for person J to take £999,910 for herself and for each of the others to take £10 each. This is outcome 2, and they all prefer it to outcome 3: £10, after all, is £10 more than nothing, even if it is less than £1 million. If these were the *only two possible outcomes*, because J is a brutal dictator, for example, then outcome 2 would be 'Pareto-optimal' and would be selected ambiguously by the Pareto Principle. Everyone is better off under outcome 2, and they all prefer it.

The fact that person J probably prefers it much more than the others cannot be taken into account by the Pareto

Principle, since to do so would involve making an interpersonal comparison of utility. However odd this result looks, the fact remains that outcome 2 is preferred by all to outcome 3 *if, and only if, only these two outcomes are feasible.* In such circumstances it makes sense for the group to choose it.

If the oil barons could share the money out in whatever manner they like, however, many other options open up. One would be to share it equally, with each taking £100,000 (option 1). Nine people *very much* prefer this outcome to outcome 2. One person, J, is considerably worse off. But the Pareto Principle cannot take this into account, since it involves making an interpersonal comparison of utility. If only outcomes 1 and 3 were on the table, of course, all would rate outcome 1 higher, and the equal share-out would be Pareto-optimal. The Pareto Principle, however, cannot help us decide between outcomes 1 and 2. While nearly all prefer outcome 1, one person does not, and the Pareto Principle cannot be used.

This may seem to be a relatively minor drawback. After all, why not use the Pareto Principle when the necessary conditions are fulfilled, and use some other method of deciding when they are not? Apart from the major problem that the necessary conditions are fulfilled only rarely, the trouble with this position is that *it is possible to know whether or not the conditions are fulfilled only if all of the viable options are on the table for consideration.*

Putting all of the options on the table for simultaneous consideration is easy enough in theory. In practice it is almost impossible. In the first place, decisions involving the distribution of a *divisible kitty* of resources allow for a virtually infinite number of possible allocations. (Try, for example, to list each of the different ways in which a £1 million kitty can be distributed between 10 people, in amounts of £1!) Even with issues that have a limited number of resolutions (many moral reforms, for example), the number is still usually so large that we can consider only a few at a time.

This presents an effectively insuperable problem for the use of the Pareto Principle as a decision rule in public policy-making. It is almost of the essence of most policy problems that there are many, many potential detailed solutions, very few of which can ever conceivably be put on the table at the same time. Even leaving aside the vast number of policy problems with budgetary implications (and these, of course, create a version of the kitty-dividing problem), very few of those that remain present *only* a very limited number of choices. Thus, in practice, it is almost impossible to know whether another, Pareto-superior, alternative is not just around the corner. Worse, it is impossible to know whether an alternative that is *neither better nor worse*, in Pareto terms, is lurking out of sight. If it appears, what do we do?

The problem is that, if we'd have known about the new alternative in the first place, then the Pareto-optimal alternative would not, in fact, have been Pareto-optimal. And it wouldn't have been selected. In effect, we will discover retrospectively that the valid conditions for using our social-choice criterion did not apply.

Let's say that we had decided to develop nuclear power as a response to the energy crisis of 1973. Everyone at the time agreed that nuclear power was better than the energy crisis. Imagine that someone now perfects a solar-power satellite capable of beaming solar energy back to earth at low cost. All would have preferred this to the energy crisis, had they known about it. Most of the population prefer solar energy to nuclear energy, but some do not. In such circumstances Pareto will not allow a switch to solar energy. Nuclear energy is retained, in effect, because of the 'accident' that it happened to be considered first and then sat there on the table as a *status quo* that no other option, in Pareto terms, was capable of dislodging.

This example highlights two very serious matters. The first can be thought of as the 'problem of the *status quo*'. The second is the 'problem of agenda-setting', of deciding which outcomes are considered at any given time. Both problems tend to make the use of the Pareto Principle either conservative or perverse when it is not indecisive.

The problem of the *status quo* is the most straightforward. Most policy decisions involve the consideration of potential moves away from the *status quo*. This includes all situations in which, if *no* decision is taken, *something* will happen. And this something can be thought of as the *status quo*.

In other words, while practical decision-making involves deciding between a limited range of options, the *status quo* infiltrates nearly all sets of options, even if only implicitly, as the consequence of a non-decision. The result of including the *status quo* among a limited range of options, and of then applying the Pareto Principle to these, is that a non-decision results unless an option can be found that dominates the *status quo*. And the *status quo* then lives to fight another day. This is why the Pareto Principle is inherently conservative, rejecting even the most popular reforms if they fall short of *universal* approval.

The problem of agenda-setting is more complex. Since only a limited range of options can in practice be considered at one time, the process that is used to select options for consideration is clearly critical. Thus, if an early option is selected as Pareto-superior to some others, it may subsequently be very difficult to dislodge. Remember that the Pareto Principle gives what amounts to a veto to anyone who does not like a new alternative, since it does not allow a single person to be made worse off. Now, there may be quite a few alternatives that the Principle cannot decide between, because each makes some better off and some worse off. The *first* of these to be selected will be impossible to defeat, using the Pareto Principle. (This is a version of the problem of conservatism.)

If, for example, a group of us go rambling around looking for a restaurant in which to eat, and if we use the Pareto Principle to decide which restaurant to choose, then we may be in for a miserable evening. We may well end up at almost the first restaurant we come to (chosen by us all in the first instance because almost any restaurant is better than none). The *corden bleu* cuisine around the corner will remain tantalizingly out of reach if only one person doesn't happen to feel like eating there. If we'd settled on the *cordon bleu* restaurant in the first place, we'd have ended up there. In short, the *order* in which we consider the restaurants has a major effect on the decision we end up making. And, if I can control that order, I can have a major impact on the result. If I want to eat at the Greasy Spoon and can contrive that we visit this place first, I stand a good chance of getting my way if I appeal to Pareto. In short, the Pareto Principle favours those who *currently* have the power to influence the agenda of options. This is another reason why its practical operation will tend to be conservative.

Notwithstanding all of this, Pareto does help us to weed out policy options in certain circumstances. If one policy dominates another in Pareto terms, the policy that is dominated can be safely rejected. There is no argument for retaining the dominated policy. For example, imagine that there are three possible policies on the general running of schools. One is to have *only* private schools; one is to have *only* state schools; and the third is to have a mix of the two. The two main social groups in the community concerned rate these policies as follows:

|  | Group A | Group B |
|---|---|---|
| State only | 1st | 2nd |
| Mix | 2nd | 1st |
| Private only | 3rd | 3rd |

The option of having *only* private schools is dominated by the other two. We can safely reject it, using the Pareto Principle, in favour of *one or other* of the alternatives. But we have no basis for choosing between what is left.

To summarize, the Pareto Principle is fine in theory but not very useful in practice, other than as an initial filter. It works only when there is an outcome that dominates all others, a matter that can be settled only when all other outcomes have been considered. This rarely allows a final decision in practice and can never happen when outcomes involve the allocation of divisible resources, such as money. Using the Pareto Principle as a filter for all possible results, we may reduce the work to be done by other decision criteria. Using the Principle to select one from a *subset* of all possible outcomes produces results that can be perverse and tend strongly to be conservative.

## The Utility Principle

The monumental problems that face us if we try to apply the Pareto Principle in any useful or interesting decision-making context forces us to confront the problem of comparing the utilities attached by different individuals to the same outcome.

Go back to the problem of dividing £1 million between ten people. One solution might be to give it all to one person. Another solution might be to divide it into ten equal shares of £100,000. As it happens, £100,000 is an awkward sum of money to win these days, though few would refuse it. If you're young, it's not enough to allow you to give up working for ever; £1 million, however, is still *quite* enough to form the basis of a life of idle luxury. One of the group might argue, therefore, that the total utility of the group would be at its highest if she were to get the whole £1 million rather than letting it be divided equally. She might accept that nine extra people would be made happy by the equal-shares solution but might claim that she would be made so happy by the life-changing £1 million that this would more than compensate. What incentive does she have to tell the truth? Even if she does tell the truth, how do we evaluate her argument? How can we compare quite *how* happy various sums of money will make her with quite how happy other sums will make other people? We must face the problem of making interpersonal comparisons of utility.

We can solve the problem if we can come up with some sort

of yardstick for comparing the values attached to the same thing by different individuals. Such a yardstick is sometimes called a '*numéraire*' and, if a commonly accepted *numéraire* is available, the problem of conducting social evaluations of outcomes is straightforward. It involves some form of social accounting process, whereby first the evaluations of each individual are denominated in the *numéraire* and then a routine cost-benefit calculus is performed. However – and especially if we take the broad view of individual evaluations that incorporates vicarious consumption, spillovers and so on – it is clear that no mutually acceptable *numéraire* will be available. The problem becomes one of identifying the best yardstick or set of yardsticks, or of rejecting the whole enterprise as unsatisfactory and looking for an alternative (bearing in mind that the main alternative is the Pareto Principle, which we have just rejected). Thus, in practice, debates over the application of the Utility Principle boil down to debates over the appropriate handling of different types of *numéraire*.

There are two ways forward. The most straightforward method, and the one used by economists, is the 'revealed-preference' technique. This technique, as the name implies, allows people to 'reveal' their 'real' preferences for things by the ways in which they act. The basic idea is that the more somebody is prepared to give up, or to do, in exchange for something, the more she must want it. It is a technique that permeates much economic and political thinking.

For example, if a protest group is prepared to risk arrest and imprisonment to further some cause, we tend to assume that they feel more strongly about it than a group that merely writes a stiff letter to the paper. King Solomon used the revealed-preference technique when ascertaining which of the women before him was the mother of the disputed child. The woman who was prepared even to give up the child in order to save its life was presumed to feel more strongly about its welfare and hence presumed to be its mother.

Stated in these general terms, the method is eminently plausible and appeals to the intuition of most people. Most of us are impressed when others make huge sacrifices in order to get something and tend to assume that they must want it very much. The problem with applying the method *systematically* in order to compare the strength of feeling of two individuals, however, is that we need some *numéraire(s)* in which to denominate the sacrifices that people make.

One widely used *numéraire*, of course, is money. Those who defend the 'free market' as an efficient social-choice mechanism argue that what it does is to allocate goods to people according to how much money they are prepared to pay, and that those prepared to pay most must want things most. Thus in a situation in which some people valued vintage motor cars while others valued tropical holidays, the free market would give both the motor cars and the holidays to those who most wanted them. Each would reveal their preferences by offering something in exchange and would reveal more intense preferences by offering more. Strictly speaking, money is not essential to this process, and a market can be based on barter. An implied notion of *numéraire* still underlies this, since the goods that are to be bartered must obviously be valued by more than one actor. Alternative *numéraires* may indeed emerge, as is the case with tobacco in prisons or with staple goods (such as sugar or nylon stockings) during wartime shortages.

There are three basic, and rather obvious, problems here. The first is that money is not a good *numéraire* in practice; the second is that real markets are not free; and the third is that even free markets handle only a very limited subset of the various aspects of value that we have considered. They don't handle spillovers; they don't handle vicarious consumption; and they often handle options rather poorly.

The failings of money as a *numéraire* are obvious and arise from its unequal distribution among, and differential evaluation by, different people. It is obviously preposterous to claim that only those who pay thousands of dollars or pounds for open-heart surgery can be presumed really to want it, or that those who do not pay high health-insurance premiums are not concerned about their health. Only if money were evenly distributed and universally valued would it function as an efficient *numéraire* in a social-choice mechanism. And it is neither. This is not to argue that money does not operate as an effective medium of exchange. It clearly does. But it is to argue that we should not make deductions about individual preferences from the social exchanges that we observe.

If money is evenly distributed, or if we are dealing with very small sums that all can afford, then it does have some value as a *numéraire*. People who argue against totally free social services, for example, often claim that nominal charges serve to discourage flippant use. Some forms of flippant use (of public libraries, for example) may do little harm, but others (such as people riding around in buses for the sake of it) might be worth discouraging if they cause unnecessary congestion. In such circumstances nominal charges may do the trick, and small sums of money may function as a useful means of filtering out those who do not really value a service at all. The key, however, is to keep nominal charges at levels that all can reasonably afford to pay. Then all may reveal their preferences by paying, and money may be used as a *numéraire*.

The second problem with the market as a social-choice mechanism is that it is intensely susceptible to manipulation because in practice it is never free. All markets tend towards monopoly over time. Large, powerful operators can often adjust market conditions to their own advantage. Crucially, market prices, particularly those of staple goods, reflect free exchanges of value only in the sense that anyone is free to starve to death if she chooses not to eat.

The problem of monopoly is a version of the problem of uneven distribution and arises from one very inconvenient property of money as a *numéraire*. It can be hoarded and accumulated, given to others or passed from generation to generation. This means that inequalities tend to magnify themselves over time, and it undermines the usefulness of money as a yardstick for making interpersonal comparisons of utility. Again, the fact that money can be accumulated makes it very useful for many purposes. But it makes it disastrous as a *numéraire* in a social cost-benefit calculus.

An even more fundamental problem with the market as a social-choice mechanism, and one to which I will return, is that it can handle only a very limited subset of the various possible aspects of value. It can handle direct consumption, for example, but is poor on almost everything else. This is the problem of market failure and applies even if every condition for the successful operation of a free market is fulfilled.

In other words, a person's market behaviour reveals some information about the value that she attaches to direct consumption benefits but reveals much less information about other benefits that she derives from an action. An obvious example concerns options. As we saw earlier, many people derive option value from a public transport system, even if they never use it. They will feel sad if it is withdrawn, yet nothing of this aspect of their preference is revealed by their market behaviour. As far as the market is concerned, they don't buy the public transport, and they give no indication that they value it in the slightest degree.

There are, therefore, severe problems in using the market as a social-choice mechanism and hence in regarding market outcomes as in some senses reflecting a social rationality. Some of these relate to markets in general and some to the specific interpretation of money as a *numéraire.* As far as money is concerned, we might seek alternative solutions.

Time, for example, might be regarded as a *numéraire* with more desirable social properties than money. Everyone, after all, has the same number of minutes in the day and the same number of days in the year, so that the inequality problem seems less severe. Furthermore, time is much more difficult to stockpile than money. In order to consider time as a *numéraire* in which people reveal their preferences, we need to assume that people value things at least in rough proportion to the amount of time that they are prepared to devote to achieving them.

This is not to say that unequal power relationships cannot be denominated in time. After all, the powerful person often demonstrates her power by keeping lesser beings waiting. How long A is prepared to wait for B often says quite a lot about their relative power. The most striking example of this phenomenon can be found in the interminable hanging around that people claiming social welfare benefits are subjected to.

None the less, time does seem better than money in a number of ways, a matter that throws new light upon an institution that most people either ridicule or revile: the queue. A queue effectively functions as a way of making people spend time to get something. It is therefore a preference-revealing mechanism. (A queue is also a rationing mechanism – as is money – but I will not consider this aspect of it here.)

This is the reason why queues can be very useful to policy-makers who are trying to estimate aggregate social preferences. Indeed, it implies that policy-makers might do well to maintain queues for policy outputs precisely in order to help them identify the things that people value most. When two services are available at equivalent levels of supply, the service generating the larger queue must be the one that is the more highly valued. It is interesting to note that when money-based markets are suspended (for example, by ration coupons in times of war), then queues are usually a by-product of this. Obviously the relationship between supply and demand needs to be taken into account when assessing the usefulness of a queue as a preference-revealing mechanism.

Thus money is not the only possible *numéraire* in which individual preferences can be denominated and aggregated. In any situation in which demand outstrips supply, we can expect to find demand-revealing behaviour of some form or another, and some of this may be generalizable enough to be capable of being reduced to a *numéraire*. Notwithstanding all of this, money-based markets are clearly among the most important social-choice mechanisms in operation in the West, and they provide one solution to the problem of combining individual into social evaluations. While the market, as we conventionally see it, is but one form of revealed-preference system, all such systems boil down, one way or another, to a process of forcing people to give something up in exchange for something else. They all boil down, therefore, to a form of trade and can be thought of as 'market-like' in this very general sense. This means that all revealed-preference techniques suffer from some of the general failings of the market, most notably that they fail to capture all aspects of value.

The alternative method of seeking a utility-based method for the collective evaluation of outcomes rests on the notion of 'posited preference'. This notion attempts to get around the problem that people can reveal preferences only in terms of a range of imperfect and unsatisfactory *numéraires* by making a set of very sweeping assumptions. By and large, it is the method used by those who analyse 'rational' policy-making from a political science perspective, and it tends, in practice, to mark one of the main distinctions between political and economic approaches to the same policy problem.

The first sweeping assumption that is usually made is that some underlying notion of utility can in practice be adopted to characterize the evaluations of the same thing by different people. Ultimately this assumption must ignore the powerful tautological argument that this is simply not possible. The solution, however, is to proceed as if it were possible. This can be justified in terms more of the alternatives than of first principles. The primary alternative, the revealed-preference technique, moves from the proposition that no general *numéraire* of value is perfect to the solution of looking at the actual *numéraires* that people reveal by their behaviour in the real world. The drawback is that the real world is a very imperfect place in which it is difficult to distinguish between people's preferences and their power. The posited-preference situation accepts the theoretical impossibility of using any commonly valued underlying notion of utility, then goes on to do it anyway on the supposition that, whatever the theory, in practice it does make sense to talk in terms of common standards of value.

The second sweeping assumption that must be made by

posited-preference techniques is that it is possible to propose a set of statements about the specific ways in which people put value on things. Not only do we need to assume that there is some underlying *numéraire* in which people can denominate their preferences, but we also need to assume things about what those preferences are. This usually is a monumental step, though it does have the great advantage that it enables us to test hypotheses about the rationality of people's decision-making. Given assumptions about what an actor wants, we can observe how she goes about getting it.

In short, the revealed-preference technique looks for the *real-world numéraires* in which people actually express their preferences and makes sweeping assumptions about the common evaluation of these. The posited-preference technique sets up a *hypothetical numéraire*, 'utility', and makes sweeping assumptions about the ways in which people denominate real-world outcomes in terms of utility.

The two approaches, for example, would handle the phenomenon of queues for various policy outputs quite differently. As we have seen, the revealed-preference technique takes the queues as given and uses different queueing behaviour to infer different evaluations of different outputs. The posited-preference technique would assume the various evaluations of the outputs that people were queueing for and would use these to explain observed variations in queuing behaviour.

The posited-preference approach enables us to explore possibilities and is, thereore, a very valuable heuristic tool for the theorist. For *practical* applications of the concept of rational decision-making, however, it seems to me that we need to be very confident about the motivational assumptions that we make before we can justify the use of posited-preference techniques. And even when we are confident, the pay-off (an investigation of the rationality of decision-making) is not spectacular in this context. On the other hand, as I indicated in chapter 3, we may *for practical purposes* assume that decision-making on policy matters is rational in its own terms and may use the revealed-preference technique to throw light on the motivations and preferences of those who have an input into the decision-making process.

As I have just emphasized, the preferences that are reflected may well be those of power-holders rather than of the group as a whole, and we must be careful how we generalize. We will, therefore, be capable of interpreting variations in policy outcomes between cultures only in terms of the different attitudes entrenched in the dominant ideologies of the systems concerned rather than in the general population. Nevertheless, this seems to me to be a useful exercise and one that justifies the use of the revealed-preference technique.

We must obviously proceed with caution. However, the existence of common standards of value is one of the things that is often held to characterize a coherent community. A community, after all, is a group of people who can be assumed to think in broadly similar ways, and one implication of this is that community members tend to apply broadly similar standards of value to the same things. On this interpretation, attempts at making interpersonal comparisons of utility would indeed be fatal if we attempted to compare the evaluations of a Martian and a Connemara farmer. But they would be much more appropriate if we set out to conduct a social evaluation on behalf of a community of Martians (or, indeed, of Connemara farmers). Within such a community it does make some sense to say things like, ' "People" put such-and-such a value on the benefits of good summer weather (or the disadvantages of an unwelcome spaceship).' Indeed, this very phenomenon is one of the important benefits that people may be thought to derive from belonging to communities. When you are a member of an established community, you feel secure because you know how others think. You can therefore predict their behaviour and thus conduct your social life from a position of relative confidence about the outcomes of your social interactions. When you move to another community, you feel somewhat at sea because you don't know quite how people put a value on things. In short, it is my claim that the existence of a feeling of community implies at least *some* interpersonal comparability of utility schedules.

*Within* a community, therefore, it should be possible to conduct some form of social cost-benefit analysis, on the basis of broadly agreed yardsticks, in order to evaluate social options. *Between* communities yardsticks will differ.

## The Aggregation of Diverse or Uniform Opinions

Before we leave the matter of the making of social evaluations, it is worth noting that the fact that such evaluations *can* take place within communities does not mean that they will be uncontroversial.

In the first place, any social cost-benefit calculus will involve the aggregation of a number of individual evaluations that are based on a range of *numéraires*. Such evaluations will also be based on a range of trade-offs between these, on a wide variety of subjective estimates of the probabilities associated with various outcomes, and on a range of quite different attitudes to the discounting of future costs and benefits. In the second place, while some 'overall' or aggregate evaluation of an option may emerge in one direction or the other, this may be the result either of a broad consensus or of the balancing out of a range of quite different views. An option may be rated as having *no* net costs or benefits, for example, as a result either of the unanimous indifference of the whole group or of a delicately balanced set of intense views for and against. And the two options, of course, generate quite different political problems.

I have just argued that the existence of a community imposes coherence on the range of possible variations in the evaluation of public costs and benefits. It is only by making such an assumption that we have been able to move forward at all. Yet we should not assume that because people talk a common language of analysis they will therefore agree on their conclusions.

Consider the debates taking place over the future role of nuclear power in both Britain and the United States. Now, most of the protagonists agree *broadly* on the yardsticks they use for evaluation. Most of them agree on the need for a large-scale electricity generation, for example. Those who do not agree, and who advocate major cuts in living standards to reduce electricity consumption, can be thought of as being 'out of the mainstream', not quite part of the community. The same might apply to those who advocate the use of nuclear energy in order to weaken the industrial power of the mining unions in Britain. While there is broad agreement on this criterion, there is, however, radical disagreement both about the subjective probabilities of possible scenarios and about the discounting of these outcomes over time.

Thus anti-nuclear campaigners assign far higher subjective probabilities both to the costly accidents that may result from a nuclear power policy and to the likelihood of finding cost-effective alternative power sources. On the accumulation of nuclear wastes, supporters of nuclear power are more sanguine than their opponents. This is sometimes because they discount future costs much more steeply and sometimes because they assign a far higher subjective probability to the discovery of a permanent method of dealing with nuclear wastes, even though no such method exists at the moment. Arguments on both sides rely heavily on the judgements of technical experts to lend weight to predictions about future scenarios.

In the same way, the time horizon adopted can lead to quite different conclusions about the present-day role of nuclear power. If a longer time horizon is used, then the long-term search for alternative power sources looks more attractive and the long-term build-up of nuclear waste may seem more worrying. Even while agreeing on most technical matters, two groups could still come to quite different conclusions on the basis of different attitudes to time discounting.

A measure of the controversy reflected in the combination of any set of individual preferences into some form of social aggregate will be the diversity of the different evaluations that are taken into account. Consider two recent constitutional issues in the Republic of Ireland – the introduction of a constitutional ban on abortion, and the constitutional provision for the extension of voting rights to EEC citizens. Referenda on these issues were held in 1983 and 1984 respectively, and each had a majority in favour. However, the constitutional ban on abortion aroused strong emotions on both sides, while that of extending voting rights aroused intense apathy. The net evaluations of the two issues might have looked rather similar, but they couldn't have been more different in terms of the range of views that each reflected. On the abortion issue a moderate net evaluation in favour of the constitutional ban resulted from the subtraction of the intense views of those against from the intense views of those in favour. On the voting rights for foreigners issue the same moderately favourable evaluation was the result of a moderately favourable view held by nearly everyone who was not totally indifferent.

Any aggregation procedure masks a lot of the diversity that exists in what has been aggregated. Two private companies, for example, make each maybe a profit of £1 million in a year. Yet one may make it on a turnover of £1 billion and the other on a turnover of a mere £2 million or so. The profit made by each is the same at the end of the day but means something very different in the first case (which might well be seen as a disastrous failure) as opposed to the second (in which the profit represents a riproaring success).

When arriving at social evaluations this matter is crucial, particularly given the problem of making interpersonal comparisons of utility. The moderate approval of a policy that results from a range of intensely conflicting views is, of course, more worrying in this respect than one that arises from a coherent range of views that varies only from apathy to vague approval. When intense views must be offset against one another, the *precise* arbitrary assumptions that we must make in order to do this are much more critical. Slight changes in these assumptions can easily reverse the result. In the case of the more coherent set of modest preferences, almost any set of assumptions that we might make on trade-offs and the like will produce more or less the same result.

This is an argument for using a measure of the *diversity* as well as of the *aggregate* of individual preferences to inform collective decision-making. While almost no formal system of decision-making does this in theory, in practice much informal social decision-making operates on the basis of allowing effective vetoes that can be mobilized by groups that feel strongly enough about an issue to do so.

A good recent example was the threatened 'rebellion' by British Conservative back-bench MPs over the issue of cutting state support in the form of grants to the better-off parents of university students. Protecting the interests of well-to-do constituents (who, of course, were a very small minority of the population) the Tory MPs threatened to vote against their own party on the matter. The row attracted considerable media attention, and the Government backed down. It did not back down because it feared defeat in the House of Commons – it could almost certainly have forced the measure through. Rather, one presumes, it backed down because to ram the measure through in the face of intense opposition from its own supporters would have been politically embarrassing. In other words, the *informal* rules of the social decision-making process (dealing with matters such as political embarrassment) accorded an effective veto to the rebels.

One important factor that affects the level of the diversity of preferences that can be found in any system concerns the manner in which the views of individuals on an issue interact with one another. Many of our preferences are not absolute but are instead conditional, in some senses, upon the preference of others. People may well *anticipate* the results of a collective evaluation when forming their own individual evaluation, rather than proceeding as if no one else existed. In so doing, of course, they modify the very collective evaluation that they are anticipating.

Consider the decision that is to be made by a workforce about whether or not to go on strike. Each individual may have a 'private' view about this. Many views, however, may be conditioned by whether or not people expect the strike to be successful. And this expectation, of course, depends upon the views of others. The more who favour the strike, and the more strongly they favour it, the greater the chance of its success. What this means is that, while the social decision is based on individual views, those views are conditioned by the anticipated social decision. And what *this* means is that the views of individuals interact with each other.

The process of debate that sometimes preceeds a decision in this type of case is thus a crucial part of the decision-making process. It is during this process that private views are revealed, thereby allowing *conditional* preferences to be firmed up, as people are able to see which way the social wind is blowing. Thus a strike can be a success or a failure in large part because people believe that others believe that it will succeed or fail. And their preferences about taking strike action will be conditioned accordingly.

## Putting a Social Cost-Benefit Calculus into Operation

This book makes no policy prescriptions. It is totally unconcerned with evaluating policies as good or bad, as efficient or inefficient. Thankfully, therefore, I am spared the most intractable problem of them all, which is to specify a *precise method* for conducting a social cost-benefit calculus. It is sufficient for my purposes to argue, as I have argued above, that such a calculus – however imperfect – is at least broadly feasible.

Policy-makers, of course, will have to be much more precise if they wish to evaluate or justify policy options on the basis of a given set of criteria. It is one thing to argue, as I have just done, that a community is likely to be characterized by the acceptance of a broad set of evaluation criteria. And it is a relatively short step to argue that, if such a set exists, then a social cost-benefit calculus can be performed (though a number of new problems do arise and form much of the substance of the discipline of welfare economics). It is quite another thing to conduct such a calculus in a rigorous manner for a real policy problem. Much of the complexity of the work on 'rational policy analysis' is concerned with the innumerable difficulties associated with putting into practice the general principles that we have discussed. In many ways it is a thankless task, since every assumption specified draws a barrage of criticism, yet *some* specification is necessary if the process is ever to get off the ground.

While I will largely wash my hands of this matter, it is worth reviewing one or two examples of the process at work in order to highlight the problems involved. The field of transport policy is one to which formal cost-benefit analyses have quite frequently been applied, to both good and bad effect.

The now infamous Serpell Report on British Rail, for example, conducted an analysis of the rail network as if it were run as a private business. Very little account was taken of the social costs and benefits involved, and the conclusion was that large sections of track should be closed. The earlier Beeching Report had, of course, already been implemented and hundreds of 'loss-making' miles of track had been closed. The effect that this policy had on rural communities and small towns was felt by very many people, but these losses never entered into the calculated costs of Beeching's cuts.

Thus the easiest form of social cost-benefit calculus to which a public enterprise can be subjected is an analysis of its financial balance sheet as if it were a profit-seeking private company. The likely conclusion, when the balance sheet shows a loss, is that the enterprise has failed.

The problem is how to include other costs and benefits in a balance sheet denominated in hard cash. We inevitably return, you will note, to the problem of *numéraires*. Few would deny the social benefits that arise from rural rail services. Yet how are these to be weighed in the balance? How can we say whether the social benefits of a particular line are worth £1 million of the taxpayers' money, £2 million, £3 million, or even £100 million?

*Some* social costs and spillover effects, of course, *can* be quantified, though this is done surprisingly infrequently. A rail service reduces road traffic on all parallel routes. This reduces spending on road building and maintenance. It reduces the level of road accidents and of consequent charges on the public purse for medical care, widow's pensions and the like. It reduces levels of air pollution from car and lorry exhausts and so on. Since the link between levels of road use and expenditure on road maintenance can be quantified, a credit needs to be entered for the rail service in the appropriate account. If the line is closed, this means that real, not metaphysical, extra money will need to be spent. In the same way, the relationship between the level of road use and the level of road deaths or injuries can be established, and at least the direct financial costs of these accidents can be calculated and credited to the railway line.

In short, quite a lot of hard work can be done, even using the crude social currency of money, to 'add in' social costs and benefits to the evaluation of many public enterprises. Much will still be left out because it is not denominated in cash, and it is here that a dry-sounding subject like cost-benefit analysis can become controversial.

Consider time. Rail services often save a lot of time as compared with cars. In rush hour it takes, let's say, three and a half hours to drive from the centre of Dublin to the centre of Galway. The current rolling stock can make the rail trip in three hours, while a big investment in new track and rolling stock could reduce the journey time to an hour and a half, given rail performance elsewhere in Europe. Say that 1,000 people a day use the train at the moment. They save about 500 hours per day between them by deciding not to drive. How much is that time worth? If 2,000 people used a fast service, so that 4,000 hours per day would be saved (or about 1 million hours per working year), how big an investment is justified? It is interesting in this context to note that transport economists tend to treat travelling time as a rather different sort of time from say, leisure time or working time. One contention is that it is assumed to be worth about one-quarter of the rate of pay for the individual concerned. Understandably, there is little real agreement on the matter, but this convention would mean that if you earned £4 per hour (about the average industrial wage in Ireland in 1984), you would be assumed to value at about 50 pence the time saved by taking the existing train, rather than driving, from Dublin to Galway (thirty minutes or so saved at a value of £1 an hour). Put another way, you should be prepared to pay, on average, 60 pence more for a train that got you to Galway forty minutes sooner or £2 for one that got you there two hours sooner.

The calculation could be extended to estimate the 'time-saved' value of the high-speed rail link at £1.5 million a year, which, if the money for it were borrowed at an interest rate of 10 per cent per annum, would justify spending £15 million to improve the service in 'time-saved' benefits alone. Yet if we take quite a different view of the value of travelling time, we can come up with quite a different sum.

For example, even at an overtime rate of time and a half, people offered unlimited overtime work only a certain amount. At the point at which they refuse more work they are opting for leisure time rather than earnings at the rate, for an average industrial worker, of £6 per hour. Why should we not take £6 per hour as a revealed-preference estimate of the average value of leisure (and hence of travelling) time? If we did, in terms of time-saved alone this would justify spending £90 million, rather than £15 million, on upgrading the rail link.

The problem that this discussion highlights concerns the effects of the arbitrary assumptions that must often be made in any practical attempt to quantify all of the social costs or benefits of a real-world option in terms of a common currency. (Perhaps the most grisly examples of this can be found in the cash values put by courts, tribunals or insurance companies on lost arms, legs, eyes or even lives.) Any assumption will be arbitrary and open to challenge, even ridicule. Each assumption looks a little odd when we write it down on a piece of paper and stare at it. Yet to make *no* assumption, and effectively to ignore these elements in the social calculus, is even more arbitrary. If we object to saying that time spent on a train is worth £1 per hour or £6 per hour, why should we feel happier to say that it is worth £0 per hour?

In short, the practical application of any social cost-benefit analysis presents enormous problems, and any practical solution is open to challenge. Failing to conduct the analysis, however, is simply another (even more questionable) practical solution to the problem, which doesn't vanish if we simply pretend that it isn't there.

To sum up, the aggregation of individual preference into a social evaluation almost inevitably involves comparing the uncomparable. Yet we do it every day on the basis of a range of assumptions, be they explicit or implicit. When we lay bare these assumptions in an explicit social cost-benefit analysis, they often look rather peculiar. But covering them up doesn't make them any better. Crucially, there are ways in which we can attempt to be systematic about social evaluations of policy options, at the very least ruling out those that are dominated by others. Beyond this we may do no more than force ourselves to think about the trade-offs or the estimates of subjective probabilities that we make. There is certainly no foolproof way to proceed, but for the purposes of the rest of this book all we need to know is that social evaluations *are* made every day, however imperfectly. Once they have been made, they have an important bearing on the nature of the policy problems that each issue generates, as we shall now see.

# 8

# Combining Public and Private Evaluations

## Identifying Potential Policy Problems

When someone evaluates a possible action, there are three broad conclusions that she might draw. The action may promise net benefits; it may promise net costs; or it may promise neither. At the same time, the action can be evaluated by all others who are affected by it, and their evaluations can be aggregated by means of some form of social cost-benefit calculus. Once more, this calculus may indicate a positive, a negative or an indifferent response.

The public and the private evaluations of an action may coincide. Thus an action may generate both public *and* private benefits. An artist or an inventor, for example, may work solely for her own satisfaction, yet she may also provide considerable public benefits for everyone else as a result of her activity. On the other hand, an action may generate both public and private costs. An example is reckless overtaking. I overtake other cars only with great care when I am driving. I do this because of the potential costs *to me* of being involved in a head-on collision on a blind bend. Every other road user, however, benefits from my caution. When public and private evaluations lean in the same direction, there will be no conflict of interest between the individual actor and the group of people affected by her action.

By contrast, public and private evaluations may be directly opposed. An action may yield private benefits and public costs.

This happens every day that I pollute the environment with my car. An action may yield private costs and public benefits. This happens when I *don't* build a house in the middle of a beautiful landscape. In such cases there is a direct conflict of interest between the individual actor and the group of people affected by her actions.

In some circumstances an individual may be indifferent about an action that yields either costs or benefits for the group. As a motorist, for example, I care little whether I drive on the sidewalk or the roadway. Pedestrians, however, have strong feelings about this. By contrast, an individual may derive costs or benefits from actions with negligible public impact. This is the usual assumption made by economists about what happens when you buy apples in the market place. And the time at which I go to bed, for example, has a much greater impact upon me than it has upon anyone else.

Finally, there may be some actions about which *both* the individual *and* the group is different. All of this can be summarized quite simply. Each of the nine possible inter-actions between public and private evaluations generates different implications for public policy, though a number of these implications are relatively innocuous. When public and private evaluations lean in the same direction (interactions A and I) or when public and/or private evaluations generate indifference (categories B, D, E, F, H) there will be little controversy.

Thus there is in a sense no need for public policy when both individual and group agree on their evaluations. The relevant

| OTHERS' NET EVALUATION | ACTOR'S NET EVALUATION | | |
|---|---|---|---|
| | *Positive* | *Indifferent* | *Negative* |
| Positive | A | B | C |
| Indifferent | D | E | F |
| Negative | G | H | I |

actions will take place, or not, anyway. It is also the case that there is no need for public policy when public evaluations generate indifference. The individual will act, or not, and the group will remain unaffected.

When private evaluations tend towards indifference and public evaluations are either positive or negative, we see a crucial, if uncontroversial, role for public policy. This is the situation created by the classic co-ordination problem. I don't really care whether we all measure distance in miles or kilometres, whether we all drive on the left or right or what sort of electric plug we all use. But I can see that there are good reasons why we should all do or use the same thing. If the public evaluation is 'drive on the left', I am not in any serious conflict with the group. Actions such as these can be thought of as being costless to individuals, while they do, of course, generate benefits for the group. We tend to care less about them because of the absence of any conflict of interest, but they are crucial none the less. This is because as well as being without individual cost, such actions are also without individual benefit. This means that there is no guarantee that any indifferent individual will behave in the way that is valued by the group. If the individual is indifferent to both $x$ and $y$, yet the group wants $y$, we see a clear role for public involvement in the decision.

When public and private evaluations lean in *opposite* directions (as they do in categories C and G), then the activities concerned are unambiguously in the realm of public policy-making. Explicit or implicit decisions must be taken that have the effect of reconciling the divergences between public and private evaluations. In such circumstances the public-policy problem that is generated can take one of two forms.

It may concern the public *costs* of actions that *benefit* an individual. In this case the problem is whether or not to regulate individual behaviour. Alternatively, it may concern the public *benefits* that arise from actions that impose *costs* on the individual. In this case the problem is whether or not to engage in public stimulation, either to produce the benefits directly or at least to produce incentives that are designed to modify individual behaviour.

Regulation and stimulation present two rather different types of public-policy problem, though both ultimately depend upon the coercive power of the state. Thus the problem of pollution is one that arises when people derive private benefits and increase social costs by disposing of harmful waste products in public places. The problem of medical research, however, is often that people are not prepared to incur private costs in exchange for public benefits that are available to all. In the first example one obvious policy response is to regulate polluters. In the second it is to stimulate the research either by doing it directly or by offering incentives to others. In either case the fact that public and private evaluations conflict places the action firmly in the domain of public policy. In each case some form of central coercion is involved – either in the regulation or in the taxation that underpins a public response.

## The Scale of the Policy Problem

Once in the public domain, the scale of the problem generated will depend upon a number of things, not least of which is the number of people engaged in the activity at issue. It is very rare, of course, for us to consider policy problems generated by a single individual, and the foregoing discussion is not intended to imply this. Occasionally a single sniper or hijacker can place an entire nation in this position. Sporadically a nation responds spontaneously, through a disaster fund, to an individual tragedy. More frequently, of course, we are dealing with *classes* of action, engaged in by *numbers* of people.

The key issue here is obviously that activities generate policy problems on a greater or lesser scale according to the number of people who are involved in the activity concerned. This matter is much less straightforward than it might seem at first sight because the spillover effects of individual actions often add up in ways that are not at all proportional to the number of people who are causing the spillage.

Consider the build-up of traffic towards the early morning rush, for example. The first car on the road creates a major spillover, shattering the peace of the night. Two, three, five, ten or twenty cars more are hardly worse than one. You lie awake in bed, but the road and the jams of rush hour are still far away. The added spillover effects of the extra cars at low levels of traffic flow are relatively small. Yet each extra car steadily clocks up private benefits for the driver. Thus, in a sense, twenty cars on the road may create less of a policy problem than one. The social costs are more or less the same, yet the private benefits are twenty times greater. Yet, as additional cars join the road, spillovers such as air pollution may increase rapidly, while the likelihood of traffic jams increases proportionately. As you feed extra cars into a road, one at a time, the rate of traffic flow down the road can suddenly begin to decrease, as the maximum capacity of the road is approached and a total traffic jam becomes likely. At low use-levels of the same road, adding further cars causes no extra problem whatsoever. (There is no added congestion if a road is carrying one car every thirty seconds rather than one car every five minutes, despite the fact that it is carrying ten times as many cars. No road, however, can take one car per second in a single lane without a high risk of crashes and consequent jams.)

Social costs may, therefore, increase very slowly as more people engage in a particular activity; they may also increase very rapidly. A given activity may be such that the entrance of new actors adds social costs at a rate that can vary quite dramatically. As is the case with traffic flow, the net *balance* of public and private evaluations can shift backwards and forwards in ways that may sometimes be unexpected.

Most forms of pollution, for example, are such that low levels of activity have almost no social costs at all. This is particularly so for levels of pollution that are low enough to allow the natural environment to break down the pollutants and to disperse these safely. Once enough people are causing sufficient pollution to outstrip the environmental system's capacity to respond, however, pollution levels can build up, and critical levels, at which the entire system is threatened, can quickly be reached.

The pumping of raw sewage into a tidal estuary or basin illustrates this phenomenon quite clearly. Tidal scour may be capable of dispersing a certain rate of sewage pumping, leaving pollution levels on public beaches well below danger levels. The sewage system may be in a 'steady state' in which, while there is always a little sewage on the beaches, its overall level is not increasing. If the level of discharge increases, however, it may exceed the rate at which tidal scour can disperse it. Pollution levels then rise steadily until danger levels are reached. At certain critical levels the social cost generated by sewage is not at all proportional to the amount of activity involved.

In the same way, the controlled extraction of *renewable* natural resources can sometimes even increase the size of the resource. Controlled fishing in a limited fishery, for example, may remove threats to the stability of the system posed by overcrowding. However, if fish are extracted at a higher rate than that at which the fish stock can replace itself, the size of the fishery will dwindle. At some high level of extraction it may go into irreversible decline as the size of the remaining stock slips below some critical minimum necessary for self-sustaining survival.

In each of the above cases social costs rise rapidly at certain critical levels of activity and increase much more slowly (or even decrease) at other levels. A policy problem, therefore, must be defined by a mix of public and private costs and benefits *at a certain level of activity*.

## The Forms of Response to a Potential Problem

At any given level of activity the nature of a policy problem depends to a large extent on the balance of public and private costs and benefits.

Some problems are likely to be very clear-cut, generating massive costs on one side and tiny benefits on the other (or *vice versa*). Thus, if I wish to engage in target practice on the top deck of a number 38 bus, and if I want to pin my targets to the backs of the other passengers, few will quarrel with the idea that the private benefits of my activity do not warrant the social costs. In every political system of which I have some knowledge, the use of live bus passengers for target practice is strictly controlled and regulated. In the same way, the social costs of introducing the disease of rabies to a country are seen, in almost every system, as being so high that the private pleasure of importing that darling little puppy you found on holiday is very strictly regulated. No state, to my knowledge, allows people to import rabid dogs at will.

A vast number of policy problems that involve conflicts between public and private evaluations, therefore, are seen by most groups as quite straightforward, to be decided by an 'obvious' trade-off between public and private interests.

Any particular trade-off may indicate public regulation, public stimulation or *laissez-faire*. When an activity generates public costs and private benefits, the trade-off between these may well indicate that the benefits outweigh the costs. Inaction, rather than regulation, is indicated. Thus it is with the excessive eating of processed starch, an activity that many become addicted to but that generates significant social costs in terms of the burdens on the medical system imposed by obese people and so on. Yet the response in most political systems is *laissez-faire*: over-eating is much less of a subject for public-policy debate than, say, smoking.

Conversely, many situations may be such that private costs are seen as yielding an insufficient trade-off for consequent public benefits. Most streets, for example, look nicer if everyone paints her front windows and doors reasonably frequently. Rarely, however, is this seen as a matter for public concern, even less as demanding direct public involvement.

The typical public response to peeling paint is *laissez-faire*. This does not indicate that the problem has not been noticed; rather, it suggests that the issue is not deemed to merit public action.

To summarize, the process of defining a public-policy problem has two stages. The first stage is to define the *existence* of a problem. This process involves identifying circumstances in which public and private evaluations conflict, and it may produce different results when the same issue is evaluated in different cultures. Different aspects of cost and benefit may be considered as appropriate elements for inclusion in the cost-benefit calculus.

The second stage of the process concerns whether or not a problem that has been identified should be acted upon. This depends on a trade-off between *agreed* public or private costs and benefits. This also may produce different results in different cultures. In some societies only very low levels of public cost may be tolerated in return for a certain private benefit; in other societies much higher levels of public cost may be tolerated for the same private benefit.

### A Framework for the Classification of Policy Problems

The factors that generate potential policy problems relating to a particular issue are summarized in Figure 1. A potential problem is generated if public and private evaluations conflict. No policy problem is generated if they do not. Once a potential problem is generated, it may be recognized as an appropriate subject either for public regulation or for public stimulation. Alternatively, an explicit or implicit decision may be taken not to act or regulate but instead to adopt a *laissez-faire* response. The response selected depends upon a trade-off between public and private evaluations. This trade-off is represented by the wavy line in the figure.

For a given method of trading off public and private

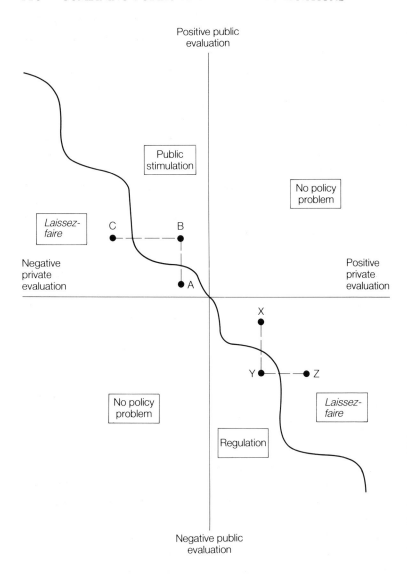

**Figure 1** Framework for classifying public responses to potential policy problems

evaluations, this line represents a boundary between activities for which the trade-off yields a net positive evaluation and those for which it yields a net negative evaluation. Thus for one action private costs may outweigh public benefits at a given trade-off rate. For another action public benefits may outweigh private costs. The two actions B and C, say, will fall on opposite sides of the trade-off line.

For a given rate of trade-off between public and private, two actions may generate the same level of private benefits, yet different levels of public cost. If they thereby fall on opposite sides of the trade-off line, they may well invoke different policy responses. Actions X and Y, for example, have the same private benefits. Yet action Y provokes public regulation because it has higher public costs, while action X 'provokes' a *laissez-faire* response. Conversely, actions A and B have the same private costs. Yet action B invokes public stimulation because it offers greater public benefits, while action A, falling on the other side of the trade-off line, results in a *laissez-faire* response. In the same way, two activities with the same public evaluations may evoke different policy responses because of different private evaluations. This is the difference between actions B and C or between actions Y and Z.

Thus within the same culture, if we feel justified in assuming that people make the same trade-off between public and private, we can compare broad public responses to different policy problems by looking at the side of the trade-off line on which they fall.

Compare two polluting activities, for example, each with broadly the same social costs. Exhaust gases can be pumped into the atmosphere either from a car exhaust pipe or from the chimney of a domestic fire. In their day both home fires and motor cars have been significant causes of atmospheric pollution around major population centres. In most industrial cities the burning of smoky fuels in home fires is now regulated quite strictly, while the pumping of car exhaust into the air is not. The availability of alternative domestic energy sources means that the net private *benefits* of bituminous coal fires are now much less than those of petrol-driven cars. Most states fix a trade-off line that bans home-fire pollution but not car-exhaust pollution. The key in this example, of course, has been the availability of cost-effective substitutes for the polluting activity. If there were no effective substitute for bituminous coal as a home fuel, the *net* benefits of coal fires would increase. The policy response would no doubt be different. Conversely, in California, where the social costs of car pollution are higher than those of most other places, more steps are taken to regulate it.

In almost any society many, many social costs are tolerated with equanimity. Figure 2 illustrates, however, the different public responses to the *same problem* that may well be adopted in different cultures. The figure shows two trade-off lines, I and II. Some activities, such as D, will be treated in the same way in both systems. This activity has very high private costs and low public benefits. Almost no public/private trade-off would indicate public action. The same situation obtains, for rather different reasons, in the case of activities G, T and W. In each case either the public or the private dimension so dominates the other that almost no trade-off is likely to generate a different policy response.

There are many, many policy problems that are tackled in broadly the same way in every culture. Quite a few of these have already been mentioned. Public health-and-hygiene regulation, for example, typically prevents people from making small private gains by taking shortcuts and thereby risking huge public costs. Thus maintaining a filthy and verminous restaurant kitchen might well be activity T. It would probably provoke public regulation under almost any public/private trade-off. National defence is typically held to produce huge public benefits for relatively small private costs. National defence might well be activity G and will always be a matter for public action rather than a *laissez-faire* response.

Consider activities E, F, U and V, however. For a group making trade-off I, activities E and F provoke public stimulation and are treated in the same way as activity G. For

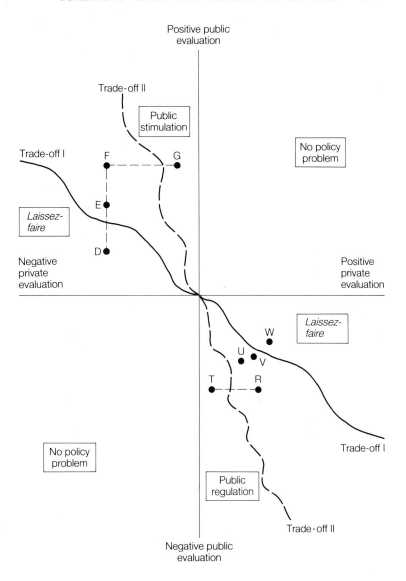

**Figure 2** Different trade-off rates

the group making trade-off II, the same activities evoke a *laissez-faire* response. They fall on a different side of the trade-off line. Yet another group might form a trade-off line that generated responses different to activities E and F. In the same way, activities U and V generate public regulation with trade-off I and *laissez-faire* with trade-off II.

This is the position of activities that move in and out of the political arena as we turn from culture to culture. Thus many US states have a *laissez-faire* response to the public costs of privately owned firearms. Most European states regulate this quite strictly. (Private ownership of firearms might be activity U.) Land-use planning is another matter that varies dramatically from culture to culture, once more as a result of variations in the position of the trade-off line that balances the public costs to the group as a whole against the private benefits to the developer of a particular building development.

Differences in the public/private trade-off line may thus generate different responses to the same problem in different cultures. Such trade-offs, of course, are products of the ideology of the group concerned. Thus even within a given culture ideological debate often concerns the matter of where the public/private trade-off line should be drawn. The closer a given policy area is to the actual trade-off line, the greater the chance that different groups will have different preferred policy responses to it. Such policy areas will thus form a key battleground for public debate, falling as they do on different sides of the public/private trade-offs made by different groups. (Personal health care, as we shall see, is a very good example of such an issue.) The further a policy area is from the trade-off line, the less likely it is to occupy this central position in public debate, since it is less probable that different groups will come to different conclusions about it.

The scheme outlined in Figures 1 and 2 will therefore apply unambiguously to the classification of policy problems for a given group only if all group members feel the same way both about public and private evaluations of actions and about the trade-off that should be made between the two. This may seem unrealistic, and indeed it is, but an ideal scheme such as this helps to identify four quite different types of controversy over public policy:

1  disputes over the private evaluations of actions;
2  disputes over the public evaluations of actions;
3  disputes over the trade-off between private and public evaluations;
4  disputes over appropriate specific responses to an agreed policy problem.

The first three disputes concern the *definition* of the policy problem; the fourth concerns its practical *solution*. It is my contention that we can gain considerable purchase on the comparative analysis of public policy by concentrating on different perceptions of the problem involved. A large part of the literature about comparative public policy, on the other hand, concentrates on specific policy responses to a given problem, about which it is inevitably much more difficult to generalize.

For a given polity we may proceed by identifying the various social groups, at least in so far as these groups differ on their public and private evaluation of a problem and on the trade-off they make between the two. The policy outcome will then be determined by the balance of forces between groups. This last stage in the process, however, is not part of my purpose in this analysis, which is concerned much more with the *range* of acceptable solutions to policy problems within a given polity than with the *actual* solution adopted. (The actual solution can depend on this, that and all sorts of other things besides.) I am concerned, therefore, to construct a framework that enables us to identify the battleground. I am not concerned, in this discussion, with trying to pick the winner.

# 9

# *Laissez-faire* as a Policy Response

We have just seen that a policy problem may generate one of three potential public responses. These are public regulation, public stimulation and *laissez-faire*. A *laissez-faire* response involves public inaction in the face of an acknowledged policy problem and results from a trade-off of public and private costs and benefits that indicates neither sufficient public costs to set against the private benefits nor sufficient public benefits to set against private costs.

The emergence of such as a conclusion is conditioned by the intrinsic properties of the activity concerned and by the particular public/private trade-off function in operation. *Laissez-faire*, of course, generates an outcome that is just as definite as that of any other policy response. More often than not *laissez-faire* outcomes will be favoured by some of those concerned and opposed by others. Thus *laissez-faire* is no different, in principle, from any other policy response. It involves doing nothing; but the fact that it involves doing nothing as a considered response to a policy problem means that it has precisely the same analytical status as the policy responses of regulation or stimulation.

In the capitalist West the adoption of a *laissez-faire* policy usually means the turning over of a problem to a solution based on the operation of existing market forces. As I have already indicated, the market is a form of social-choice mechanism. The problem is that the outcomes produced by the market are not always those that 'people' want. Sometimes, indeed, they are outcomes that *nobody* wants. This is sometimes referred to as the problem of *market failure*, and market failure provides one of the classical justifications for government action, either to *regulate* or to *stimulate* individual decision-making.

Market failure is pervasive and inevitable. A full discussion of its many forms would take up several books. The extent to which the market is or is not free in any real sense is an important aspect of this problem, though it is an aspect that I shall not consider here, given the immense literature on the subject. Even within the assumption that the market is 'free' to an acceptable degree, however, problems of market failure arise for a range of reasons. I will consider two classes of these here. The first concerns the ways in which the continuing operation of free markets usually depends upon a continuing system of government regulation and enforcement, a process that in itself is heavily conditioned by policy considerations. The second concerns the failure of markets to take account of the range of elements of value that we have already considered.

### Regulation for Market Freedom

The state regulation necessary for the continued operation of even rudimentary vestiges of freedom in a market involves three basic types of activity. The first concerns the enforcement of contracts; the second concerns the regulation of monopolies and of restrictive market practices; and the third involves the administration of some system for the apportionment of damages for market activities that injure others.

Nearly every market that is ostensibly free depends for its successful operation on a system of contracts. Very few significant deals in a free market can be consummated instantaneously. Most involve an exchange that involves one party or the other in making the first move, whether this is parting with money or supplying goods and services. Whoever makes this prior commitment will do so only in the expectation

E

that the others involved in the deal will reciprocate when the time comes. In small groups and communities trust may suffice to create this expectation. In larger groups, where the parties may well not even know, let alone trust, one another, contracts will need to be enforced.

From a thousand Hollywood B-movies, of course, we know that there is such a person as a private enforcer. From a handful of the more perceptive of these, however, we also learn that there's nothing to stop a private enforcer from enforcing a contract that never existed. Give her the means to enforce a *bona fide* contract, and you give her the means to enforce an extortion demand. The market, therefore, would be a chaotic and lethal environment if it relied exclusively on private enforcers unregulated by any public agencies. Public enforcement via some form of legal system is clearly essential. And what is distinctively 'public' about public enforcement is the involvement of the state, the Government or some other agency with the collective legitimacy to act in the interests of the group as a whole.

Now, it is sometimes thought that the enforcement of contracts is an entirely neutral process, creating, if you like, a 'passive' role for the state. On this view people make contracts, putting whatever they like into these, while the state simply enforces these terms when the parties come into dispute. This, however, is to ignore a number of crucial political features of the practical application of any system of contract law. In practice, when a contract is brought to law there are many ways in which the norms and values of the community at large may be imposed upon the contracting parties, and there are a number of circumstances in which policy considerations can be explicitly invoked. Many contracts, for example, may be void at law, while others may be subject to quite wide-ranging interpretation by the legal system. The most obvious cases of contracts that are void are those that are prohibited by statute (such as those involving price-fixing agreements or restrictive trade practices) or those that involve agreements to commit illegal acts (such as the traditional murder contract). In such cases community values, as far as these are reflected in the laws of the land, will regulate freedom of contract, and such regulation will be enforced by the state. It is inconceivable, of course, that things could be any other way. Clearly public courts can never be used to enforce contracts to break the law, and clearly the laws of the land thereby impinge upon the market. This may seem an innocuous enough point when we consider matters such as murder but has a major impact once we considered the vast range of legislation in operation in any modern state.

Contracts may also be deemed void on the grounds, among others, of mistake, misrepresentation, duress or undue influence. In actually deciding whether such factors come into play, the notion of what it is 'reasonable' to presume is often used. And what is 'reasonable' is obviously defined in large part by community values. Indeed, the notion of the 'reasonable man' is a pervasive one both in contract law and in the law of tort, to which we shall shortly be turning. In each case, however, the key point is that the interpretation of what is 'reasonable' in a given situation is not at all a matter for some sort of legal 'machine', unaffected by the society in which it operates. *Policy* considerations will indirectly permeate the enforcement of contracts in the form of 'judicial' *interpretations* of that which is considered to be reasonable conduct.

A further important element in the interpretation of a contract arises over the role of 'implied terms'. It is obviously not possible to anticipate every possible eventuality in a given contract. Unexpected circumstances are often governed by what we know as the 'implied terms' of the contract. These usually reflect 'normal practice' or 'custom' in the activity concerned. Thus, if it is usual for fishermen to put into port and repair their nets on the quayside when these are damaged during fishing expeditions, and if the nets are then accidentally destroyed on the quayside, then they are covered by maritime insurance in precisely the same way as if they had been destroyed at sea. This is true unless the insurance contract *explicitly excludes* such cover. Similarly, if I contract to sell something to you, all sorts of implied terms relating to my ownership of the goods and to their merchantable quality will be in force, even if these are not stated explicitly. Recent consumer legislation often goes further, actually declaring certain specific *exclusions* to be void, even in the explicit terms of a contract.

In short, the enforcement of contracts in practice is a far from neutral affair, often involving the application of community norms and values. In so far as contracts are essential to the operation of a market, the market itself will be subject at the very least to implicit public regulation of this form. Markets without contracts cannot operate, while those with contracts will be regulated by the state to some degree or another.

## Monopolies and Restrictive Practices

One of the paradoxes of capitalism, of course, is that free markets can operate only if their 'freedom' is heavily protected by government action. All markets are subject to a tendency towards oligopoly or monopoly, as the successful operators drive out the unsuccessful. Once inequalities between market operators exist, these tend to magnify, as larger or more powerful operators can function more effectively than smaller or weaker ones. Once the number of operators is relatively small, the prospect of cartels, or of other forms of collusive restrictive practice, is considerable. In other words, free markets function only when the number of operators is so large that collusion is infeasible, yet the relative market advantage of larger operators produces a tendency towards concentration.

It is no accident, therefore, that one of the cultural environments most favourable to the operation of the free market, the United States, also sustains one of the most swingeing systems of market regulation. Anti-trust legislation in the United States contains some of the toughest anti-monopoly and anti-restrictive practice provisions to be found in market economies. Historically this situation was at least in part a response to the emergence of the extremely powerful Standard Oil monopoly that developed in the early part of this century. In practice, regulation has a much greater impact on some areas (such as banking, which is very diversified in the USA) than on others (such as the production of mainframe computers, which is very concentrated). Nevertheless, what is regarded by many as the world's premier free-enterprise economy remains predominant largely because of a heavy dose of government regulation.

This situation calls into question the very meaning of the notion of *laissez-faire*, at least in so far as it is applied to economic interactions. Very rarely does *laissez-faire* involve leaving things completely alone. Much more frequently it involves the setting up of certain ground rules, within which activity is left alone as far as possible. Thus IBM *could* easily swallow up ICL, Britain's largest indigenous manufacturer of mainframe computers. The unadulterated logic of market behaviour no doubt indicates that it *should* do so. Freed from competition, IBM could subsequently increase its prices in the British Market. One of the ground rules of the game, however, relates to the regulation and prevention of monopolies in certain markets. The British Government would no doubt not only intervene if such a takeover were ever mooted but would intervene and regulate the market in the name of market freedom.

In the same way, bankruptcy is a routine aspect of the operation of a free market. Major bankruptcies, however, have major impacts on the economic and social systems in which they occur. The ground rules of most market systems contain implied terms to the effect that major bankruptcies of this nature will almost certainly not, in practice, be allowed to happen. Thus in one week in March 1985 both the US and the Irish Governments made major market interventions to prevent serious bankruptcies. In the USA, in the face of a major run on savings and loan institutions in Ohio State, the institutions were closed, while the Federal Reserve Bank offered financial help to the stricken companies. In the face of the imminent bankruptcy of the Insurance Corporation of Ireland (ICI), the Irish Government effectively took its management out of private hands. (ICI wrote around 25 per cent of all the employers' liability insurance in the state, and the collapse of this would have had major economic ramifications.)

We can thus see two basic contexts for public intervention to maintain the operation of 'free' markets. The first, and by far the more significant, concerns the need for free markets to be protected by government regulation. The second concerns the interaction between major events in one important area of market activity with events in another. In either case the *practical* operation of *laissez-faire* policies involves leaving things alone *within certain quite definite limits*. Either way a highly qualified notion of *laissez-faire* is involved.

## Laissez-Faire and Damage

We have already seen that one of the most important consequences of unregulated market interaction will be the generation of costly public spillovers. Few would argue that I should be responsible to *nobody* for the consequences of my private actions. Most would accept that when I cause damage to others they have a right to recover from me.

If I light a bonfire in my back garden, for example, and if the smoke from this dirties your washing, *you* suffer a loss as a result of a spillover from *my* action. In most systems you are entitled to some redress. You can bring a civil action against me for this, either claiming damages for the cost of rewashing your clothing, or seeking a court injunction that prohibits me from lighting further bonfires, or both. If I refuse either to pay or to comply, I will be in default. If I persist in this, bailiffs may be sent to seize property to the value of my debt. I may even be jailed for failing to comply with a court order. Either way physical coercion that is backed by the authority of the state will be used to regulate my behaviour.

The important point to remember is that this dispute is not simply a matter between individuals. As soon as it goes to court a form of government regulation is involved, and the pure notion of *laissez-faire* is abandoned. Damage caused to others is typically covered by the law of tort. Even more than in the law of contract, the law of tort is influenced by highly culture-specific notions of what a 'reasonable man' would either do or believe in particular situations. Furthermore, the law of tort has also been heavily conditioned by considerations of public policy. Most of the major departures from established precedent (the convention that purely economic loss is not recoverable, for example) have been made in quite explicit consideration of the implications for public policy. In short, the operation of the law of tort as a means of resolving individual disputes is a form of public intervention in private life. The specific content of that law and the principles of interpretation that it uses to resolve disputes are aspects of public policy. And, as in the case of legal contract enforcement, the actual operation of the law in this manner will inevitably bear the stamp of community norms and values.

However, a much more important aspect of the problem of leaving the resolution of damages to the courts is that many spillovers are caused, not by identifiable individuals who can be dragged into court but by the general actions of a *collection* of individuals that has no corporate identity. Continuing with the illustration of dirty washing, let me give one well quantified example, which concerns the costs of living in Manchester.* In 1918 the Manchester Air Pollution Advisory Board conducted a comparative study of weekly washing costs in Manchester and Harrogate. The extra cost, in 1918 pence, of the weekly wash in Manchester was 7½d. With a population of 750,000, extra fuel and soap costs therefore amounted to £290,000 each year. Could the problem of pollution have been solved by court actions against the polluters?

---

*This example is cited by Richard M. Titmuss in *Social Policy* (London: George Allen & Unwin, 1974), p. 61.

Even if 7½d. a week was sufficient cause for a court action for damages, against whom should a Manchester resident bring this case? The residents themselves, of course, were doing most of the polluting by burning coal in their fire places. No individual could be held responsible since no individual action would make a blind bit of difference to the level of pollution. This form of smoke pollution, of course, was a classic problem of collective action, since only if all stopped burning coal would any citizen benefit. It was a problem that the civil courts, in practice, would have been helpless to resolve.

If I had seen myself as an injured party, even the most avid of free marketeers could hardly have advised me to attempt to obtain nearly 200,000 court orders, one against each coal-burning household in Manchester. For this reason alone, leaving aside the problems that would have faced the judges in apportioning any specific blame, the solution offered by the law of tort would have failed.

Thus we see that not only does the law of tort depend to a considerable extent upon interpretations of notions of reasonable behaviour, and not only are rules of law determined to quite a significant extent by public policy considerations, but many forms of spillover, especially those that are widely distributed, are unlikely to be dealt with in practice by the courts. In short, we see once more that *laissez-faire* is conditioned by relatively explicit ground rules, deriving as often as not from relatively explicit policy considerations.

## The Failure of Markets to Deal with All Aspects of Value

More conventionally, the problem of 'market failure' is held to concern the inability of markets to take account of all aspects of value. We have already seen that spillovers, for example, are imposed on people regardless of market forces. Indeed, market interactions often positively encourage the selection of options with higher levels of damaging spillovers if these are more cost-effective when measured in pure cost-benefit terms. Typically, action taken to reduce spillovers is costly, and such costs will be avoided by any who are not forced to pay them. The only market mechanism likely to reduce the level of pollution from automobile exhausts, for example, would involve an increase in the price of petrol, leading to pressure towards its more efficient combustion. Equally, a reduction in the petrol price is likely to lead to more profligate use and, consequently, higher levels of pollution.

We have also seen that market forces are unlikely to generate positive spillovers when these involve private costs. The spillovers of research into preventative medicine, for example, are enormous. The private benefits of research into a commodity that cannot be sold, however, are likely to be insufficient to render it cost-effective in pure market terms.

Spillovers, of course, are aspects of the *public* evaluation of a particular activity. Therefore, it should not be all that surprising that the private market cannot deal in them. However, not only do markets deliver only by accident those outcomes that are efficient in terms of *public* evaluations, but they also typically fail to take into account many *private* aspects of value. Consider both vicarious consumption and options.

By and large, a limited 'market' in vicarious consumption value is sustained in most societies. Indeed, it is remarkable how closely the market in which charities operate, for example, resembles the market for the supply of *direct* consumption benefits. Charities advertise; they compete with one another for resources; and they hire professional public relations agencies and fund-raisers. They must also, of course, compete with other private producers. It may seem a little cynical to say that charities sell vicarious pleasure, but this is certainly one way of looking at them, and those who are in the business of raising money for charity ignore this interpretation at their peril.

We are all confronted with a continuous stream of requests for charitable donations. Few can afford to give enormous amounts to each charity. Most of us must choose between our charities in rather the same way that we choose between different brands of soap powder. We give, I suppose, to the ones that we feel give the best vicarious value for money. We are influenced, as I mentioned earlier in my general discussion of vicarious consumption, by a range of factors that colour the intensity of our interest in the welfare of others. Many of these factors, furthermore, would appear to be quite similar to the factors that influence our spending on private consumption. Particular advertisements, particular newsreel shots, particular types of tragedy attract much more interest than others. This is despite the fact that many of the others, if we were to give the matter any serious thought, would no doubt seem just as worthy. In short, the level of impulsive market behaviour, and the benefits to suppliers who can package their product to take advantage of this, are at least as high for vicarious goods as for any other.

When vicarious and direct evaluations of a particular action lean in the *same* direction, the market can often satisfy both. When they have responded to recent 'Buy Irish' campaigns, for example, Irish consumers have been able both to buy goods that they would be buying anyway and to derive additional vicarious satisfaction from providing employment for Irish workers. This may serve to make Irish goods more valuable than other goods to Irish consumers, and it may even lead them to be prepared to pay a higher price for Irish goods as a consequence. The 'vicarious premium' consists, of course, only in the *added* cost of the Irish goods. Provided that this is not excessive, then they may well seem a good buy. The greater the premium, however, the fewer the people we would expect to avail themselves of it. Few consumers would buy Irish at *any* cost.

When direct and vicarious evaluations lean in *opposite* directions, however, the market can be a very inefficient way of distributing value. Consider the market in Christmas cards, for example. The fund-raising use of Christmas card sales by charities produces a very confusing situation for the Christmas card consumer. Christmas cards, of wildly varying quality and price, are marketed both by private entrepreneurs and by charities. The charity card comes with a clear vicarious bonus – some or all of the profits will help the needy somewhere. Faced with identical Christmas cards at an identical price, most consumers would therefore choose the charity card, since it gives them more value. Only the most miserable misanthrope would do the reverse. Charities may well try to push up the price of their cards in order to extract a somewhat greater return for the vicarious satisfaction that they are, of course, selling. So far so good: we have conventional market behaviour. When charity Christmas cards are of poorer quality than those of the private entrepreneur – and, alas, this is sometimes the case – then the consumer in search of vicarious value can find herself in a difficult position. Her direct and her vicarious satisfactions run in opposite directions, yet the market is forcing her to buy both as part of a single package, represented by the charity card.

She may, for example, decide to buy the charity cards yet not use them, and to buy better cards on the private market to send to her friends. This would be grossly inefficient. She would get still more vicarious satisfaction from simply *donating* the price of the cards to the charity, which could then raise even more money, since it would not have to produce the cards or, having produced them, could sell them to someone else. If she buys the cards and doesn't use them, both the charity cards and the resources they represent go to waste. Similarly, if the seeker after vicarious value cannot afford both to buy good cards and to give the price of another set of cards to charity, she may instead buy poor-quality cards at a lower price in the private market and send the balance to charity. In this case the charity cards remain unsold and their production costs are wasted.

We are conditioned, of course, to take a higher level of interest in others at Christmas. Demand for vicarious goods increases at this time, and the charity cards step into the market. When charities produce high-quality cards, no conflict arises. When they produce poor-quality cards, inefficiencies are caused by the marketing of direct and vicarious satisfaction in the same product.

Returning to 'Buy Irish' campaigns, we see another clear example of this type of potential inefficiency. The purchase of Irish butter involves at most a very small premium. Buying only Irish coconuts, however, would involve spectacular costs, in terms either of price or of quality, and would represent very poor vicarious value for money. In short, when the markets in direct and vicarious value overlap on the same commodities, there is absolutely no guarantee of efficiency.

Option value, another crucial element in any private cost-benefit calculus, is not always handled efficiently by the market. Thus it can often happen that a private company goes bankrupt, yet nearly everyone regrets its passing. A good example is that of a delicatessen located in a town that was just a little too small to keep it in business in terms of day-to-day trade. People were delighted to see the delicatessen open, for two reasons. Some regularly shopped there, buying valued goods that were otherwise unobtainable. Many others, however, didn't use the shop but liked to know that they *could* have bought all of those exotic foreign ingredients should they have wanted to do so. Many of these people never bought a truffle in their whole life. However, when they read the recipe for *pâté de foie gras truffé*, it made them happy to know that they *could* buy a truffle in the delicatessen and *could* cook this should they ever decide to do so. When the shop closed down, these people felt a sense of loss, even though they had not once bought a single item of exotic food in it. Their *option* to use the shop had been removed, and they felt much worse off as a result.

Thus options are valuable, and people may well be prepared to pay quite a lot for them. Very often, however, the market does not give them a chance to do so, or at least it does not give them a chance to do so with any real hope that their payment will be effective.

Moderate users of a delicatessen, for example, may buy more exotic goods than they need, simply to help to keep it in business. Even non-users who are relatively confident that they will use the place in the future may buy the odd truffle as their contribution to its continued operation. But the market provides no mechanism for ensuring that these voluntary option payments are devoted to the purpose for which they are made. Indeed, it offers no mechanism for the effective extraction of such option payments at all. The owner of the delicatessen could go knocking at the doors of her non-customers, threatening to close down if they did not each give her £5. It is unlikely that anyone would give her money on this basis or that, if it were given, there would be any guarantee that anything would be provided in exchange.

A version of this problem underlies the trend towards monopoly in any market that deviates from absolute equality among all operators. Once one producer offers a cheaper commodity than her rivals, for example, consumers buy from her. The rivals lose business, and if, because of some market imperfection or another, they cannot compete on equal terms, they go out of business. Competition dies, and the remaining producers form a cartel and increase prices. Individual consumers cannot be expected to buy from more expensive producers simply in order to keep these in business and to preserve the competition that keeps overall prices low. The options that consumers have function to keep prices down. When people fail to exercise these options, prices may rise. The very real value of the options that *were* available will become apparent once they have disappeared. Yet the free market offers little scope for dealing in these.

## Conclusion: the Consequences of Impurity

Just as there is no such thing as pure *laissez-faire*, so there is no such thing as a totally free market. What we have instead is a policy response that amounts to allowing *particular* market forces to allocate social resources. Crucially, such market forces must often be protected by very heavy doses of government regulation before they can operate at all.

Thus go-getting video entrepreneurs campaign vigorously for government action against pirates, and the state is in great demand from the private sector as protector of copyrights, patents, licences and franchises. Meanwhile, if major airlines are even suspected of conspiring to lower their prices in order to force a newcomer out of business, then someone held up as the epitome of the swashbuckling private entrepreneur will take them to court and sue them for unfair business practice. To buy shares in a company when you *think* a takeover bid is about to be launched makes good business sense. To buy the same shares when you *know* the takeover will be launched will probably be illegal in many systems because it amounts to insider dealing.

The list goes on and on, but the essential feature of these examples is that they are not examples of intervention by those who believe in a mixed economy and wish to superimpose welfare considerations on the logic of market interaction. They are examples of the minimum levels of government intervention that are necessary in order for a market to operate at all. In other words, the market these days is not something that just happens if Governments do nothing. Contemporary 'free' markets are monitored and nurtured and protected by Governments. The *particular* market forces that are tolerated must therefore be viewed as considered policy responses to a given problem, since they exist, almost always, under the explicit auspices of a particular regulatory regime operated by the state.

The distinction between this form of regulation and the regulation that we shall be discussing in the following chapter, therefore, is one of *motive* rather than *substance*. As we have seen in general terms, regulatory policy may be used to control spillovers and to deal with other conflicts between private benefits and public costs. This contrasts with the regulation that is used to protect market-based optimization based on purely private evaluations. Once broader conceptions of private value, such as vicarious consumption and option value, are considered, the market may fail even to supply these. A further justification for public intervention is thereby generated.

The main point, however, is that *laissez-faire* must be regarded as an active policy response, reflecting a particular public/private balance based on a particular set of trade-offs. Only very, very rarely are even the biggest barracudas in the market in favour of a fully fledged *laissez-faire* environment. Typically, they favour a particular form of public intervention that reflects a heavy general emphasis in favour of direct private costs and benefits and a heavy particular emphasis in favour of big barracudas.

# 10

# Public Regulation, Public Stimulation

## The Interaction of Regulation and Stimulation

We should not set too much store by the distinction between regulation and stimulation. As often as not, these policy responses are two sides of a single coin. In the first place, Governments frequently move in to produce a service directly because the private sector will not produce it when subjected to a set of regulations introduced to further some public policy objective. If private carriers would deliver letters to remote islands for the same low price as they might deliver letters from city centre to city centre, for example, the logic of public participation in the postal service of every Western nation might well be different. In other words, the regulatory solutions to a whole range of policy problems are such that only the state is prepared to deliver in accordance with its own regulations.

In the second place, the distinction between a public producer and a private producer whose every action is subject to public regulation can be rather slim in practice. For example, there are, doubtless, significant differences between British commercial television companies and the BBC. However, these differences are rendered very much less marked by the regulatory role fulfilled by the Independent Broadcasting Authority (IBA). The commercial companies are forced to maintain less popular programming, which attracts lower advertising revenues (documentaries, for example), and end up offering a range of programming that really is very little different from that of the BBC.

In the third place, when Governments do act as the direct producers of services, they typically protect a monopoly position for themselves on the basis of the direct prohibition of competition. This enables unprofitable services to be cross-subsidized by profitable services and prevents private entrepreneurs from creaming off income from profitable services and leaving loss-making services non-viable. This, of course, is a standard policy response to the public provision of transport services. Very frequently low-demand routes with a high social value (rural bus services, for example) are subsidized by profitable high-demand routes (urban commuter services, for example). This type of cross-subsidization can be achieved by price regulation of a private market, of course, as it is in the international air transport industry, but is certainly one policy justification for a protected public monopoly in a particular market sector.

In short, direct government action and regulation often go hand in hand, while other forms of public stimulation – the use of explicit subsidies, for example – are rarely free from regulation. None the less, the framework that we have used indicates whether the primary justification for, and the subsequent dynamic of, a particular policy initiative is regulatory or stimulatory. The impact of regulation or stimulation may, of course, be to generate secondary policy problems demanding different forms of response. For the purposes of discussing general features of these forms of policy response, however, it is useful to consider them separately.

## Forms of Regulation

We saw in the previous chapter that *laissez-faire* policy responses can typically be attempted only when they are circumscribed by quite a complex regulatory regime. Regulation to enable *laissez-faire* responses is not, however, designed to ensure the control of actions with private benefits and public costs. It is with this latter form of regulation that the following discussion is concerned.

In general, Governments regulate individual behaviour either by explicit coercion or by a system of penalties (backed up, of course, by the coercive power of the state). Polluters, for example, can be either directly prevented from discharging harmful waste products or fined for doing so. Both techniques are used, but coercive prevention, however easy in theory, is in practice considered such a swingeing response that Governments are not always willing to follow through with the consequences.

If a polluting factory fails to respond to a demand to curtail its noxious outpourings, for example, it can be closed down or it can be taken over and run by government nominees. This is often seen, however, as rather like using a sledge hammer to crack a nut, a solution that most Governments would be prepared to justify only in terms of the most extreme environmental costs.

A much more common policy response is to impose fines on the factory. For a fine to be effective, however, it must be large enough to act as a deterrent. And for this to be the case the level of the fine, discounted by the probability of detection and punishment, must exceed the benefits of continuing to pollute.

One of the tragedies of pollution, for example, is the fact that the social costs that it causes are often vastly greater than the private cost to the polluter of treating her waste products. While the social costs tend often to be spread more thinly than the private benefits and tend therefore to be less visible, pollution is generally very inefficient in social terms. Total social costs normally far exceed total private benefits. The reason for mentioning this is not to open up a can of worms labelled 'social efficiency', which is best left to the welfare economists. It is to make the point that few polluters would be able to pay fines that reflected the *cost* of their pollution. Polluters, in short, can cause much more damage than they could ever pay for. Fines, therefore, *must* be seen as methods of deterring pollution rather than as methods of covering the costs that they cause.

Since a large part of atmospheric pollution these days comes from domestic sources, whether motor cars or solid-fuel heating appliances, let us calculate the level of fines necessary to deter the burning of house coal in a smokeless zone. Say that the extra cost of smokeless fuel is £100 a year. Somebody considering burning house coal estimates that there is a one-in-twenty chance of being caught and convicted for doing so in the next year. The fine must be set at £2,000 before it will act as a disincentive. If the fine is £1,900, the potential polluter would do better to bet against a one-in-twenty chance of 'losing' and would thus do better by polluting. The expected loss arising from polluting is £95 (one-twentieth of the £1,900 fine). The expected loss arising from burning smokeless fuel is the (certain) additional expense of buying the fuel, £100. Note that this is a very pessimistic view of the chance of being caught. In reality, the chance will almost certainly be much less and the fine needed to deter pollution correspondingly higher. Note also that the imposition of a £2,000 fine for burning house coal in a smokeless zone, barely adequate as it is as a deterrent, would almost certainly be regarded as utterly draconian were it ever to be imposed.

Another example of the role of low fines in the regulatory system concerns the problem of uninsured car drivers. All Western societies now require some form of third-party motor insurance, since the uninsured motorist provides the classic case of the person who can cause much, much more damage than she can pay for. In this sense the uninsured motorist is someone who spreads what we might think of as 'risk pollution', exposing all and sundry to unwelcome risks of uncompensated damage. However, given the high levels of inflation in insurance premiums in recent years, given the fixed limits to fines that exist in most systems and given the fact that uninsured driving is an offence that is difficult to detect until it is too late, the incentives to break the law have been mounting.

Indeed, in Ireland, where premiums are very high and fines are very low (typically much less than a single year's premium), the level of uninsured driving has recently reached epidemic proportions.

Despite the unrealistically low level of fines for many violations of regulatory policy, and in particular for pollution-related offences, Governments usually prefer this form of regulation to direct and coercive intervention. An established set of legal procedures exists for trying cases, for setting fines and for enforcing these. Coercion, should it be necessary, is one stage removed from the scene of the 'crime', being invoked to enforce payment of fines rather than to regulate behaviour directly. Since direct physical intervention can be controversial, most Governments prefer to leave it to the courts to enforce fines and hence to provide the coercive teeth of their regulatory policies. Coercion, when necessary, nominally punishes the offence of defying a court order – though, of course, the order itself is typically no more than a statement of the regulatory policy.

A further method that Governments can adopt to implement regulatory policy involves the use of some form of licensing system. In such situations a Government assumes control over a particular area of activity – the classic example is broadcast-ing – and then allows only licence-holders to operate. The licences that the Government issues are invariably full of conditions, and failure to comply with these conditions renders the licence forfeit. In this way Governments can regulate on the basis of their monopoly control of a particular resource. By entering into contractual relationships with users of the resource, particular provisions can be specified and reinforced. Monopoly control means that a Government can dictate the terms of the contract and can thus regulate activity in the area concerned.

The licensing of mineral resources is a particularly good example of this particular method of implementing a regulatory policy. Especially in the case of costly off-shore oil exploration, a large multinational corporation might well be inclined, other things being equal, to stake a claim to a potential oil field but then to refrain from developing it. Particularly in an oil glut, the company may be much more concerned to secure long-term reserves, and to prevent competitors from gaining access to these, than it is concerned to engage in the expensive exploration and extraction of oil during a period of low world prices. For those countries that have access only to expensive off-shore oil (for example, Britain, Ireland or Norway), this rational behaviour on the part of international oil companies may well not serve a view of the public interest that is more concerned with reducing national dependence on imported raw materials. It is almost always the case, therefore, that off-shore oil exploration licences contain contractual obligations to bore so many test holes in a given period and to develop any viable oil discoveries according to a certain schedule. In this way regulatory policy is enacted via the licensing system, since the licences become void, and revert to the state, if their terms are not adhered to.

Land-use planning control is another policy area that generally operates on this basis. Ultimate ownership and control of all land is typically maintained by the state. The deployment of this monopoly control to implement policy considerations, relying on the leverage gained by various licences to use land, dates back to the feudal era. In a sense, modern land-use planning is merely an extension of this process, with the state maintaining the right to decide the use to which land is put and thereby implementing a system of planning permissions or licences to enforce its planning policies.

Once more, the use of licences or other contracts depends on the legal system for enforcement. Ultimately, it is non-compliance with court orders of one form or another that invokes physical coercion. Since the rule of law is a very highly valued good in all Western systems, locking people up for failing to obey the law (almost regardless of the content of the specific law or regulation in question) is relatively easy for Governments to defend. Thus legal regulation and a defence of the rule of law enables a system of sanctions to be applied in a manner that does not expose to question the particular policy objectives at issue.

What all of this goes to show is that public regulation could not succeed at all if it depended entirely on either coercion or deterrence. The costs of enforcement are too great, and the scale of the deterrence necessary in certain circumstances too large, for it to be implemented.

In practice, of course, most people obey regulations because they accept their *legitimacy*. In other words, whether or not they agree with the particular regulation concerned, they accept the right of the agency to make it, and they accept the general logic of the operation of regulatory policies. This provides an important additional dimension to policy decisions on matters of public regulation, since a regulatory attempt to move into an area that people did not accept as a valid object of regulation would be likely to fail miserably.

Regulation, in short, is much more than coercion, though coercion is always the bottom line. Regulation amounts, in effect, to the imposition of a legitimate set of enforceable disincentives in order to modify the decision calculus of individuals. The enforceability of the disincentives depends in large part on the legitimacy of the regulatory agency in the policy area concerned. Policy objectives must be determined largely by what is enforceable. However persuasive the social cost-benefit calculus, for example, it is very unlikely that any Government would ever succeed in reducing the speed limit on motorways to 15 miles per hour. And the effects of attempting to control the sale of alcohol in the Prohibition era are, of course, legendary.

## Stimulatory Responses by Government

We have just looked at the policy responses available to Governments facing problems that arise because of activities that are beneficial to *individuals* but costly to the *group* as a whole. When activities that benefit the *group* as a whole are costly for *individual* group members, Governments face a rather different set of problems.

Direct regulation of individual behaviour may still be relevant. The generic example concerns conscription in wartime. When volunteers do not come forward in sufficient numbers to fill the ranks of the armed forces, people may be forced to join up in the face of extreme physical sanctions. When the same soldiers decide that it is time to go home, they can be forced to remain on the battlefield, dead or alive.

Direct and coercive forms of government response to this type of problem, however, are the exception rather than the rule, despite the fact that they could theoretically be employed in many other circumstances. Public works such as roads or hospital buildings could be constructed by a conscripted labour force. Every member of a local community could be forced to fall in for dustbin duty once a year. However, the only major form of conscription that most Governments use, other than that into the armed services, is conscription into jury service. (In one or two systems, such as the Australian, people are also conscripted into the act of voting at elections.) The jury service example is interesting in that it is usually considered to be a fundamental principle of the administration of justice that juries represent a cross-section of the population as a whole. People who might prefer to opt out of jury service would probably make up an unrepresentative group, leaving the residual pool of jurors unrepresentative as well. Thus fully representative juries can be achieved only by the direct coercion of all, regardless of who actually *wants* to serve. The same argument could be extended to elections if it were held that the fundamental objective of an election was to assess the views of an entire group. In practice, elections are usually seen in the West as a means by which individuals secure the representation of their private views, and thus as an activity from which they may justifiably choose to opt out.

A much more common policy response in circumstances in which socially valued activities are not individually cost-effective, however, is that Governments attempt to stimulate an activity somehow or another. They may proceed in one of two basic ways. Either Governments may produce the output directly, or private incentives may be offered to individuals in order to make socially valued outcomes individually cost-effective. The incentives themselves may take one of two basic forms. The first is the straight cash transfer, in which people are either paid grants or given tax rebates in order to do certain thing. Good examples from the housing field include housing improvement grants in Britain and mortgage-interest tax relief in Ireland, Britain and the USA. The second (increasingly common) technique is the government guarantee. Loans may be guaranteed by a Government when individuals are unable or unwilling to put up sufficient collateral. As we shall see, the US Government sometimes guarantees housing loans for low-income groups. Payments to or from overseas customers may be guaranteed if international litigation presents an unattractive prospect for exporters. In issuing a guarantee, however, the Government is also making an effective cash transfer, since it is providing, for nothing, a guarantee that would otherwise have to be paid for, and often paid for quite dearly, in the private insurance market.

Whether producing directly or offering incentives, however, Governments must raise the necessary resources. Such revenue-raising is, of course, ultimately coercive and is based on some form of taxation. The coercive element in taxation is inevitable, since the justification for government activity in the first place is that the activities at issue are not produced as a result of voluntary individual action.

The coercion implicit in tax-based stimulatory policies is no less coercive because it is one step removed from the policy objective involved. It is perfectly possible to end up in prison for implacable resistance to the paying of taxes, and the tax-striker may well end up sharing a cell with a draft-dodger. Indeed, refusal to pay taxes and, ultimately, imprisonment are sometimes used as forms of protest at particular policy outputs. These are tactics that have been used, among others, by Irish-language activists in Ireland in protest at the lack of programming to be found in the first official language of the state on RTE, the official state broadcasting network. Nevertheless, the tax-financed production of either services or incentives often separates the coercion from the policy objective quite significantly. This means that stimulatory responses, *in practice*, present quite a different public face.

The precise complexion of this face depends, among other things, upon the nature of the link between tax-gathering and public spending. The relationship between public income and public expenditure, of course, is one of the key political issues in most Western systems. This is a vastly complicated subject and not one that it is appropriate to discuss in detail here. In relation to the potential responses to particular policy problems, however, it is worth making a few general points.

When Governments either produce services directly or offer a system of incentives, outputs may be made available to all or to only certain targeted recipients. If they are made available to all, this may be because of the intrinsic nature of the good or service involved. Thus we cannot easily target clean air or improvements in public health or hygiene. Alternatively, services may be made available to all as a matter of public policy. Thus Britain's National Health Service is available to all British taxpayers. But state health services can easily be restricted to certain groups, as is the case in the USA or Ireland. In addition, government outputs may be used either by all or by only a subset of the population. Some goods and services, such as clean air or defence, are *compulsory* in the sense that, once produced, all must suffer or enjoy them; others, such as roads or parks, are *optional*. Such differences become significant when considered in relation to the methods used by government to raise revenue. These take three basic forms – taxation, user charges and deficit spending – though each is a complicated subject in its own right.

## Tax-Based Policies

Taxation, of course, takes a myriad forms, but we can usefully consider the distinction between *general* taxation, designed simply to raise public revenues for government expenditure, and the taxation of *specific* activities, such as that of maintaining a car on public roads. Once again, this distinction is only a matter of degree. After all, in one sense income tax is no more than a tax on the specific activity of earning money, while non-owners of motor vehicles pay motor taxes implicitly when they buy goods that have been delivered to shops by road. Many taxes that masquerade as specific taxes on certain activities must really be seen as a form of general taxation if the activities concerned are essential to life; a sales tax on basic foodstuffs would be a good example.

The key point, however, is that taxes levied on specific activities over which the actor does have a genuine freedom of choice combine two functions. In the first place, they raise revenue. In the second place, they provide a system of incentives and disincentives to action. Good examples of the dual role of specific taxes can be found in tobacco taxes generally and in the high level of sales taxes on motor cars in Ireland. Tobacco taxes raise huge revenues for both the British and the Irish Governments, most of which are credited to the general tax account. They also serve to deter smokers. Indeed, raising tobacco taxes is usually defended on grounds not of revenue but of public health. In this case the two roles are, of course, contradictory. If tobacco taxes succeed totally in deterring smokers, they will fail completely as sources of revenue.

In the same way, high sales taxes on new cars in Ireland raise revenue for the Government and fulfil a role in the balance of payments policy. Ireland has no indigenous motor industry, and the balance of payments would suffer badly if car sales, and hence car imports, were to rise rapidly. And they would rise if taxes, and hence prices, were lowered. In this case the disincentive elements of the tax are probably at least as important to policy-makers as those related to revenue-gathering.

The second important general element in the policy implications of tax-gathering concerns whether particular taxes are deployed for *general* spending purposes or are earmarked for *specific* budgets. One of the best examples of earmarked revenues in days gone by was the Road Fund, a product of taxes levied on motorists and used explicitly for road-building. In the United States this is still generally the case, but in Britain and Ireland motor taxation has long since been absorbed into the general tax fund, while direct spending on roads is now much less than tax payments by motorists (though it may well not be less than the overall public costs of motoring, including pollution, road deaths and so on).

Earmarked tax funds may be based on either general or specific taxes. The road fund is an example, still relevant in the USA, of a specific expenditure fund based on a specific, and directly linked, tax. Recently some Western Governments have used earmarked portions of levies on tobacco advertising to fund anti-smoking campaigns. Other earmarked funds may be based on general forms of taxation. The recent Youth Employment Levy in Ireland is a good example. The levy is effectively a general 1 per cent income-tax surcharge, but funds thus raised are used exclusively for youth employment projects.

By far the most common form of tax-funded public production, however, takes the form of the non-earmarked funding of general public expenditure. There is, then, no direct link between general tax income and specific public expenditure on individual projects. This lack of a direct link between income and expenditure is a key feature of public production. It frees public spending from market forces and must be considered a positive virtue, since the failure of market forces is the justification for public action in the first place. It may also, however, be a liability, particularly if alternative mechanisms for the effective control of expenditure on specific projects are not introduced. That the breaking of the link between income and expenditure is both the justification for, and the ruination of, many public projects will be a matter with which most people are very familiar. We have grown accustomed to crazy cost over-runs on capital projects that seemed eminently desirable when first mooted. This matter lies at the heart of the debate about public policy in most systems. The obvious reason for this is that non-market mechanisms for the control of public expenditure must be based upon clearly specified criteria, while the clear specification of such criteria will inevitably cause intense controversy.

One of the main reasons why the specification of criteria for the effective control of public expenditure will be controversial relates to the distribution of the benefits of public spending. Most production will distribute benefits unevenly, either because it is targeted at specific groups, as we have seen, or because the services provided are *taken up* at different rates by different people.

One of the most dramatic examples of this process concerns the supersonic airliner Concorde. The operation of Concorde's supersonic transatlantic passenger services is not economically viable on simple market criteria. Huge public write-offs of the plane's development costs have been necessary, constituting a massive subsidy of the service from general tax revenue. Concorde carries little commercial cargo that might be used by a wider public. Its fares are very high, and therefore it carries mainly rich people. Take-up of the huge public spending encapsulated in Concorde is thus very limited and concentrated in a small minority group. The spending, of course, is funded by all. Concorde therefore may almost have achieved the status of a generic example in its own right by now. It certainly is a very good example of the redistributive effects of tax-financed public production, in this case a dramatic redistribution from poor to rich. Concorde, however, is only an extreme example of a general and inevitable situation. Any bridge, road, bypass, hospital and even lighthouse that is constructed benefits those who use it much more than those who do not. Even if some benefits – reduced freight transport costs, for example – spill over to all, the general distribution of benefits is both uneven and unrelated to the distribution of costs.

Much debate over the nature and funding of government production, therefore, is rooted in competition between groups of potential consumers for public expenditure that specifically benefits a particular group but is paid for by all. This is one potential reason for the steady growth in public spending that has been observed in all developed countries during the course of this century, a growth that is very largely unaffected by changes in the ideological complexion of the Government in power. There is a clear potential for individual subgroups within a society to be 'bought off' by policy concessions in certain areas that benefit the few but are paid for by all. Each individual concession makes the few very happy, yet appears to cost the many very little, as costs are spread very thinly. Each, therefore, may seem politically expedient. It is only when specific policy concession is piled on specific policy concession that public spending rises inexorably and a form of collective action problem is generated. The collective-action problem arises because each valuable concession to an articulate, powerful or troublesome few may not be felt as an additional burden by the tax-paying many.

It is important to note that this does not provide an argument against tax-financed public production *in general*. Rather, it provides an argument against allocating public production on the basis of competition between vested interests. In general, funding specific projects from general taxation will always be a controversial process. If such projects are responses to market-failure problems, it should not be forgotten that other versions of the problem of collective action may arise in their place, particularly when political pressure is used as a surrogate for market forces.

## User Charges

Some public expenditure is funded on the basis of direct charges to users. This is particularly important for optional goods and services, such as public broadcasting, which users clearly indicate that they value by opting voluntarily to consume them. Conversely, of course, non-users indicate their low valuation by opting *not* to consume. The clear temptation is to argue that if anyone should pay for an output, then at least those who choose to consume it should pay.

The obvious problem here is to decide the level at which service charges should be set. Only in the purest of free markets, almost never encountered in practice, is there likely to be a price that is in any sense 'natural'. Furthermore we must, of course, acknowledge that the very reason for government involvement in the first place is usually that uncontrolled market prices produce outcomes that have unacceptably high social costs. There is little sense, therefore, in a Government's involving itself in the production of a particular service and then attempting to price its outputs in a manner identical to that of the market.

In addition there is a major problem of pricing caused by the fact that government involvement in production *distorts* the market, generating a price structure that is rather different from that which would otherwise obtain. A clear example of this is the government provision of public rented housing. Building resources and other factors of production are diverted to the public construction sector. This may create a scarcity of, and hence a higher price for, private building land, for example. Conversely, public house-building reduces the overall level of unsatisfied demand for housing and hence the potential rents for private housing. By reducing the pressure of private builders for land, it may even set up a countervailing pressure on land prices. When all of these various influences have interacted with one another, the private housing market will be a different place. Its price structure will be distorted by the operation of the public sector. It makes no sense at all, therefore, to take private-sector rents as a basis for evaluating public-sector rents. If the public sector did not exist, private sector rents would be different.

This is an important problem. In theoretical terms, when public-sector prices are *below* the 'true' price (whatever that means), some form of subsidy to the consumers affected is involved. When prices are *above* the true price, some form of levy or tax is being imposed. Thus in order to investigate the redistributive effect of public-sector pricing policy – clearly an important issue – some sort of valuation must be devised that reflects the price that would prevail if the public sector were not there. This is referred to as the 'shadow price' of an output.

Shadow prices are also important when we are evaluating the inputs to public-sector activity. To calculate the true social cost of building an airport, for example, we need to know what the cost of the land would be if the airport were not being built. This will certainly be lower than the market price of the land that obtains when someone is trying to buy a large block of land on which to build a runway. Calculating shadow prices is always a complex procedure, involving clusters of sweeping assumptions. But some notion of the shadow price of a good or service is necessary before we can even begin to evaluate the ways in which the public-sector price structure redistributes welfare.

Shadow prices are another major preoccupation of welfare economics that we will not concern ourselves with here. Assessing these is inevitably a controversial business, but assume for the moment that we could conceivably satisfy ourselves as to the 'true' price of a public output. If the actual price charged is below this, then a subsidy is involved. (This is almost certainly the case with transatlantic air tickets on Concorde, for example.) If the actual price charged is above this, then a levy is being imposed.

This whole issue recently came to a spectacular head in Britain in connection with London Transport's 'Fares fair' policy of rail- and bus-fare cuts, instigated by the Labour-controlled Greater London Council (GLC). This policy resulted in the GLC's being taken to court by the London Borough of Bromley for violating the Transport (London) Act 1969, which lays down the aims of London Transport as being to 'promote the provision of integrated, efficient and economic transport facilities and services for Greater London'. The key issue in the various judicial interpretations of this (culminating in one by the Law Lords) concerned the meaning of 'economic'. The outcome was that the Law Lords accepted that an economic transport system was one in which income matched expenditure on the balance sheet. It should by now be clear, of course, that this is much too narrow a definition, ignoring many of the components of value that are considered in earlier chapters. In addition, however, we should note that the Law Lords' judgment ignores totally the concept of shadow pricing. If London Transport did not exist, a quite different structure of transport costs and prices would prevail in London. Without going into these shadow prices in some detail, who is to say whether the operation of London Transport is economic in the sense that its prices cover its costs?

In short, therefore, the funding of public spending by user charges may generate a system of implicit taxes and subsidies that are just as real and important as those that are more explicit. A great problem, however, arises in evaluating these. To do this public prices must be compared with some sort of 'true' price, and assessing that true price is necessarily a complex matter. Surprisingly, it is a less controversial matter than many in the realm of public policy debate. This is because it is usually ignored completely, so that people often unthinkingly accept actual market prices as in some sense 'true' prices. Before deciding whether the tenants of public housing or the passengers on public transport receive implicit subsidies or face implicit levies, however, the assessment of true prices is a matter that must be given serious thought.

## Deficit Financing

The final element in the funding of government production is the budget deficit. Taxes and user charges contribute to government income, but almost no national Government these days covers expenditure entirely out of income. Nearly all run a budget deficit. This deficit can be handled principally in two ways. The first is borrowing, and the second is inflation.

Once more, both the public-sector borrowing requirement and inflation are immensely complex subjects, but the key feature for our purposes is the link between the funding and the output of government activity. The costs of both may be paid by people who are quite distinct from those who receive the benefits.

A few simple examples may make the point. High levels of government borrowing have two important effects. They create a burden of debt repayment in future years, and they increase interest rates by reducing the supply of money available for borrowing by others. (Both of these have dozens of other side-effects – on the exchange rate, hence on the inflation rate and so on.) The seriousness with which future liabilities are viewed depends on how people discount utility over time, a matter that we have already discussed. One important phenomenon, however, is the fact that most public borrowing is sanctioned by politicians, and most politicians take a rather short-term view of such things. While Harold Wilson's famous statement, 'A week in politics is a long time', may be something of an exaggeration, the fact remains that few current Finance Ministers expect to be in office five or ten years' hence and clearly have some incentive to saddle us with long-term public debt if this solves short-term political problems. There may thus be a real conflict of interest arising from the quite different attitudes to time-discounting prevailing among those who incur public debt and those on whose behalf it is incurred.

The level of interest rates in the economy also has an important redistributive effect, operating in a complex range of conflicting directions. High interest rates harm high net borrowers most. At a domestic level the highest net borrowers tend, in practice, to be the better off, since by far the biggest loan that most people incur is their house mortgage. In Britain and Ireland most home loans are funded by building societies. In practice, most building societies take deposits from a large number of (generally poorer) people and lend to a smaller number of those who are generally richer. In this sector, *taken on its own*, therefore, high interest rates redistribute, on balance, from rich to poor. It is an interesting consequence of middle-class control of the mass media that increased interest rates usually evoke the headline 'Bad News for Home Owners' rather than 'Good News for Building Society Depositers', despite the fact that the latter are more numerous.

On the other hand, higher interest rates may put some businesses at risk, threatening redundancies. And redundancies tend to come first from the blue-collar, rather than the white-collar, workforce. All in all, the level of interest rates has a very complex set of redistributive effects on the economy, but one thing is clear: very little attention is paid to these effects when new public spending is funded via new public borrowing. The effects of the funding are now at least two stages removed from the effect of the related spending. This makes loan-financed government production rather less immediately controversial. *With respect to a specific project*, the effects of loan-funding are usually too complex to be spelled out in the simple terms of most public debate. While government indebtedness *in general* may easily be perceived as a potential problem, a little more debt for a worthy project may often seem a tempting option – especially since the important matter of who pays the price may be well obscured.

Broadly, the same argument applies to inflation. Since the government controls the supply of money, it can solve short-term funding problems by increasing the money supply. If the money supply increases at too high a rate, this causes inflation (though arguing about what rate is 'too high' is one of the major pastimes of macro-economists). Inflation is an implicit tax on money that operates as surely and as effectively as a deduction from your pay packet. (Indeed, it operates more effectively, being almost the only tax that it is impossible to evade.) It therefore redistributes more from those with more money. Of course, those with the most money are not necessarily the richest. The rich often have little money at all (in terms of cash or bank balances), preferring goods or investments whose value rises with inflation. Nevertheless, when Governments fund public production by increasing the money supply and thus increasing inflation, they are also redistributing resources. Once more, there is a discrepancy between those who pay for public products and those who benefit from them. Once more, the rather indirect effects of inflation make the link between the cost and benefit of a *specific* public project rather hard to make.

In general terms, therefore, public production based on deficit financing, whether this is covered by borrowing or by increasing the money supply, tends to spread costs in general but obscure ways. When such expenditure benefits a limited subset of the population, we face an acute version of the potential collective-action problem of public expenditure. If spending is allocated in terms of some form of political market place, there will be a temptation for each subgroup to push for benefits that it alone receives but for which all pay.

It is worth repeating in conclusion, however, that the breaking of the direct link between income and expenditure that is a consequence of the direct government production of goods and services does not inevitably result in some form of public market failure. When Governments move beyond the economic market, some set of allocation criteria must be used for both costs and benefits. These will inevitably be controversial, and disputes over them will inevitably occupy a central role in public policy debate. And such debate will not only concern who *should* get the benefits and pay the costs, in some senses a straightforward, normative matter, but it will also revolve around the more complex technical issue of who *actually does* pay and receive how much. To answer these questions properly, we must specify what would have happened if the public sector had never existed, a daunting and contentious task, to say the least.

# 11

# Applying the Framework:
# Health and Housing

It is not my intention in this book to get into the specifics of particular policy debates. These are dealt with in expert fashion by many other authors. In order to develop some of the flavour of how this approach to the comparative study of public policy might be applied, however, I will spend a little time discussing its application to two policy areas: health and housing.

Both health care and housing evoke quite different responses in different policy systems, and both tend to be quite central to public policy debates within a given system. Each policy area, of course, comprises a vast complex of different but interacting problems. This highlights one of the main benefits that may be gained from using an appropriate general framework, which may enable complex problems to be broken down into more manageable analytical components.

## Public and Private in Health-Care Policy

In practice, of course, there are two quite separate activities involved in the provision of health care. There is the (usually) 'preventative' activity of public health care, and there is the (usually) 'curative' activity of personal health care. Both activities are often aimed at the same goal. Thus we can either attempt to dissuade people from smoking or we can treat lung cancer. We can vaccinate the population against smallpox, or we can treat the disease once it breaks out. Each of the two activities, however, has quite different social and economic properties. Public health is the quintessential example of a service that cannot be marketed in any conventional form. Personal health care, on the other hand, is a service that can be marketed very easily in just the same way as can hairdressing or manicures. Indeed, when we start looking at hypnotists, 'health' books, herbalists and 'health food' shops, we quickly see that there is nearly always a private fringe market in any health system.

In order to organize the discussion, I shall consider public health and personal health care separately, though it should always be remembered that these activities often address the same basic set of problems.

## Public Health Care

Of the policy areas that we shall be considering, public health is almost certainly the least controversial. This is because the public benefits, the private costs and the trade-offs between the two are widely accepted, and very few people are likely to disagree with the view that a public health programme is a good thing. To do otherwise is rather like declaring public support for either murder or the Devil. I have, of course, used public health examples quite frequently in the earlier discussion, usually as illustrations of activities that must inevitably be conducted by government if they are conducted at all.

Most public health-care programmes are not marketable. A partial exception concerns vaccination against infectious diseases, which comprises both a public and a private benefit at times when a disease is rife. At such times the personal protection arising from vaccination is clearly marketable. Once a given disease has been brought under control, however, personal incentives to be vaccinated decrease, since the risk of catching the disease is remote. Yet if the vaccination programme is not maintained purely as a public health measure, the disease may reassert itself. By the time that personal incentives to be vaccinated are high enough, it will, in a sense, be too late, since the incentives are established only once the disease is rife. Vaccination programmes, therefore, represent an interesting borderline case between marketable and non-marketable public health outputs. However, to be fully effective they must be treated as prophylactic programmes and thus as non-marketable.

Most public health programmes, as preventative policies, yield enormous social benefits, particularly when they are compared with the other method of dealing with the same problem, usually involving very expensive curative treatment. There can these days be little doubt that, if everyone adopted a healthier lifestyle, the burden on the health services would be greatly reduced. This is particularly evidenced in relation to major contemporary killers such as lung cancer and heart disease. It is very easy to run up a bill of £1 million, say, in treating a relatively small number of people with such ailments. The same £1 million spent on health education might well save far more lives if it were effectively deployed.

In short, the fact that the public/private balance tilts inevitably in favour of the public, and the fact that public benefits are indisputably large, to a great extent takes public health care out of politics in most systems.

Within this general atmosphere of agreement as to their general benefits, health care policies can be based either on regulation or on more direct government action.

## Regulation and Public Health

In very general terms, justifications for public health regulation are generated by a whole range of collective-action problems that would otherwise have disastrous consequences for community well-being.

Perhaps the most graphic example concerns rabies, now endemic in a large part of continental Europe. In countries such as Britain and Ireland, in which rabies is *not* endemic, the disease can be prevented absolutely by ensuring that no infected animals cross national boundaries. And for islands this is also a feasible possibility. A collective-action problem arises, however, because each individual, coming home from holiday with an endearing stray puppy, for example, reckons that the chance that her *particular* pet will turn into a mad dog and bite all her neighbours is so small that the risk is worth taking. Yet, of course, if everyone thinks like this, it is almost certain that a rabid animal will be brought into the country at some time, and this will have very high social costs indeed. This is a classic problem of collective action, one that must without doubt be solved by Governments regulating the movement of livestock if it is to be solved at all. The benefits to the population as a whole are very considerable, and they are distributed generally as the pure spillover effects of the implementation of an effective system of regulation. There is no way that such benefits could be marketed.

Rabies prevention is an extreme example, but a whole range of public health and hygiene problems have a similar structure. As I have already indicated, much motoring legislation has a public health component. Nearly all of it, after all, is enacted with the very explicit intention of reducing the toll of death and injury on the roads and can be thought of as an aspect of regulatory health policy in this broad sense. The argument has been made most explicitly over the issue of the compulsory wearing of seat belts, but it applies generally to any regulatory policy designed to reduce the number of accidents causing death or injury. Thus most of us now know that drinking and driving increases the risk of killing or maiming other people. Many people do drink and drive once in a while, usually because they don't think that *they personally* are dangerous drivers. The same argument applies to speed limits, and a general consequence of a failure to regulate in this area is a higher burden on the health service.

Other regulatory activity in the field of public health concerns problems that could conceivably be solved by markets but only at unacceptable social costs. Consider the matter of food additives, for example. If a manufacturer adds a new type of sweetener to Kosmic Krunchies breakfast cereal, and if the new sweetener causes death within five years, demand for Kosmic Krunchies will dry up once the link has been established and the news gets around. But it will dry up only after many people have died.

There are three elements to this particular example. One is the vicarious displeasure that we feel about the use of children dying as a form of market feedback. Almost nobody would be hard-hearted enough to argue that, since those who have been foolish enough to eat Kosmic Krunchies will die, the problem will soon sort itself out. A second element is the time lag that often exists between the administration of potentially dangerous substances and the effects that they cause. An obvious and tragic example here is the effect of drugs on unborn children, as the Thalidomide cases clearly show. When a time lag exists, thousands may be eating something that will kill them before market feedback comes into play. The third point is the extreme difficulty of establishing direct causal links between the use of certain substances and adverse medical effects. This is usually difficult enough in strictly controlled laboratory conditions but is obviously impossible in all but the most extreme cases of poisoning in the real world, where so many things are varying at once. Regulating the testing of such additives, therefore, is almost inevitably an activity for government.

Both drunken driving and dangerous food additives are clear examples of individuals foisting severe and direct costs on to others and hence creating a need for government regulation. There can be no debate in such areas about the prophylactic role of government.

In less extreme cases the situation is less clear-cut. Two good examples concern the wearing of seat belts and the sale of 'merely' harmful products, such as cigarettes. In both cases most of the direct costs fall on the actors themselves, whether these are non-seat belt wearers who suffer severe facial injuries or smokers who shorten their life expectancy. In each case

G

there are clear indirect social costs – to the families of those who die unnecessarily, to the health services that must treat them, to 'passive smokers' forced to breathe other people's cigarette smoke and so on. These social costs, however, are also rather more indirect than, say, the costs incurred by an innocent pedestrian mown down by a drunken driver. This has tended to generate a certain amount of public debate over whether direct regulation is an appropriate government response in such circumstances.

Compulsory seat belt legislation, for example, has only recently been introduced in most European countries and not always to universal acclaim. The sale of cigarettes is still legal everywhere, though public policy on smoking is implemented via the banning of advertising and the punitive taxation of tobacco products in many systems. (This policy emerged, of course, largely by accident. Tobacco products were subject to heavy excise taxes before they were known to be dangerous. It would be more accurate to say that a new policy *justification* has emerged for tobacco taxes.) The reason for the controversy is that both unbelted drivers and smokers claim the right to take risks with their own lives, if they so desire, and object to being forced to do what other people say is 'good' for them. In such circumstances public policy arguments in favour of regulation are either overtly paternalist (in the 'we know what's best for you' vein) or they appeal to the more indirect social costs involved. These arguments will have less appeal (and the corresponding regulatory policies will be less likely to emerge) in systems that are reluctant to give weight to indirect social costs.

### Educating for Public Health

Whether or not education should be regarded as a form of regulation is a moot point, so I shall treat it separately. As a form of social control, of course, 'indirect' socialization precedes 'direct' coercion in the sequence of things. Thus health education policies usually set out to change habits and to obviate the need for regulation. Many regulatory policies have been introduced only after education policies fail (those relating to drunken driving and seat belts are good examples). Given the fact that no regulatory policy can be absolutely effective, successful education policies reduce pressure on, and increase the efficacy of, regulatory authorities.

Health education has very clearly been effective in the case of cigarette smoking. As a result of state-sponsored propaganda campaigns, the number of smokers in nearly every Western country has dropped drastically in the past few years. Another example of the effect of public health education campaigns can be found in the sudden appearance of joggers on the roads. The impact of health education has borne *directly* upon those who fear the consequences of heart disease in later life. It has also borne *indirectly* upon society as a whole, establishing behaviour such as jogging as a more or less normal activity rather than as something fanatical or even mad. In the same way, people are now much less likely to tolerate low hygiene standards in restaurants or shops, are more likely to take care over the preparation of their own food and so on. Once more, a purely public set of benefits is involved, and the regulatory function, if it is performed at all, will be performed by government.

## Action on Public Health

Medical research has public benefits that are very widely distributed. It is clearly one of the most important aspects of government action in the field of public health. The development of cures for cancer, or for heart disease, or even for the common cold would yield enormous public benefits. Of course, medical research can be, and often is, conducted by private companies. (The patent medicine, after all, is one of the older product lines in the huckster's bag.) International drug companies make gigantic profits out of successful patent medicines, which provides plenty of incentive for private medical research.

However, commercial pressures will obviously point such research in certain directions. No private drug company is likely to devote much time to testing the theory, however plausible, that the best cure for the common cold is to stand on your head for half an hour. Private medical research will tend to involve research either into medicines or into hardware (brain scanners, wooden legs or what have you) that can be *sold* either to individuals or to health services. There is very little incentive for private drug companies to conduct research into *preventive* medicine.

A large area of medical research, therefore, will be heavily under-provided by the private sector and must be funded by government if it is to be provided at all. The same applies to most other aspects of government action over public health – for example, as we have seen, the running of immunization or screening programmes. There can be little doubt that the goal of eradicating typhus, bubonic plague or smallpox will be achieved only by central government action. One thing that you never hear is the argument that these particular activities should be hived off to the private sector.

By and large, therefore, the policy area of public health is characterized by a string of collective-action or market-failure problems that must be resolved by government if they are to be resolved at all. Variations in the handling of such policy issues between systems are thus rather limited. There is little scope for disagreement over *who* should be doing such things. There is, of course, a public choice to be made over *how many* of them are done given limited resources.

### Personal Health Care

### Personal Health or Personal Health-Care Services?

There is no necessary relationship between health care and health. Even the most cursory dip into medical history will reveal a huge range of treatments that have been at best ineffective, at worst fatal. There is no doubt that, with the benefit of hindsight, people will say the same about current medical practice. Indeed, when we consider the dramatic decline in mortality rates from most diseases since the nineteenth century, it is clear that developments in the *personal* treatment of these diseases have had little effect. By contrast, it is much more common to see a steady decline in mortality over a long period in response to developments in *public* health and hygiene policy.

Many factors affect the basic level of physical health that we each enjoy. Most of these factors are social and environmental; others concern personal habits. Heavy smoking, heavy drinking, lack of exercise and overeating all clearly make major contributions to ill health. Married people seem less likely to fall ill than single people. Middle-class people are healthier than working-class people. Tendencies towards some diseases are inherited. The level of personal *health care* received, in short, is only one among an array of factors contributing to the level of personal *health* of an individual.

Notwithstanding this, the fact remains that most people believe that personal health care enhances personal health. They believe that if the level of health care is reduced, their health will also suffer. This is clearly all that matters in this respect, and there can be no denying the enormous demand for health-care services in every Western system.

## The Role of Vicarious Evaluations in the Health Market

Personal health care is a major example of the operation of vicarious criteria of evaluation. For one thing it deals with people who *are* sick rather than with those who *might become* sick. The vicarious appeal of personal health care thus exceeds that of prophylactic public health policies. People who *might* die from lung cancer as a result of heavy smoking do not yet have names, faces, families and so on. People who *are* dying of lung cancer do possess these essential attributes and thus qualify as candidates for more intense vicarious concern on the part of others.

A matter that is obviously related to the vicarious evaluation of the effects of health policy in others is the fact that few people *choose* to fall ill. While many choose to do things, such as smoking, skiing or surfing, that greatly increase the risk of illness or injury, few desire to succumb to such risks. Most people, if they were free to choose, would choose to be as healthy as possible. Variations between individuals in the level of basic demand for health-care services may be somewhat related to preference, therefore, but they are related much more to circumstance. When people need health care some disaster, major or minor, has befallen them. This, of course, enhances our vicarious interest in the health of others. Indeed, in relation to emergency medical services, the 'consumer' is often in no position to make a decision to consume at all. Such services are often administered at the behest of others or at the behest of nobody save the medical team, operating on the assumption that the consumer would decide to live if given the choice.

All of this means that while many aspects of personal health care can be marketed, and indeed often are marketed, the importance of vicarious evaluations brings important non-market factors to bear. Few wish to see the dying left to die, even if they cannot afford to pay for marketed medical services. By contrast, few would expect to be able to claim, if their lives had been saved while they were in a coma, that they owed nobody a penny since they'd never *asked* to be saved. In each case the reality of the situation is that emergency action will be taken and that subsequent decisions will relate to the allocation of the costs of this action.

In this very important respect, medical treatment is marketed quite differently from most other products. It is interesting to note that most doctors or dentists do not display price lists in prominent positions in their waiting rooms. Consumers often have only a rather general idea of the medical costs that they are incurring, although the strong-minded among them may be able to pin doctors down to more precise estimates. Nevertheless, the health 'market' is typically characterized by the fact that the bill for medical services, once it finally arrives, represents something of a unknown quantity. The effect of market forces on the price structure is thereby weakened. As often as not, pricing takes place *after* rather than *before* purchase.

Obviously, the need to take emergency medical action in certain circumstances is a major reason for the existence of such a situation (though *post facto* pricing extends far beyond medical emergencies). This illustrates very clearly, however, the effect of superimposing *vicarious* motivations on a market system geared essentially to transactions in *direct* value.

The extent to which such vicarious satisfaction is felt, of course, depends to a considerable degree on an estimation of the 'necessity' of the treatment involved. Up to a point this is an objective matter. The actual death of the patient is possible in certain situations, after all, and not in others. Beyond this point, however, judgements on the 'necessity' of treatments are necessarily intensely subjective. Sex-change operations, for example, may be regarded as absolutely essential by some, yet as a frivolous luxury by others. In so far as there are social arguments concerning the 'objective' necessity of a treatment, we find a dimension of evaluation that stretches from urgent and essential operations, such as appendectomies, to operations that may be equally complex and dangerous but are entirely matters of whim for the patient. The latter category certainly includes much cosmetic surgery, for example. While some cosmetic surgery might be justified in special cases on psychological grounds, most cosmetic surgery is flippant in the sense that neither the physical nor the mental health of the patient is at issue. Such criteria of necessity may either be strictly medical or they may include social or psychological factors, as is the case with sex change operations. Thus major disfigurements may be deemed to be socially necessary matters for treatment even when they are medically benign.

The 'objective' necessity of a treatment is a matter that is likely to bear upon the level of vicarious cost generated when the treatment is not administered. Little sleep may be lost over those who cannot afford breast-enlargement or nose-reduction operations. Much more concern may be generated by those who die because they cannot gain access to kidney machines. (Interestingly enough, 'objective' standards of medical necessity tend to be rather strict, although they obviously include death, severe pain and incapacity. There is a well-known tendency, however, for us to regard other peoples' backaches or migraines as much less serious and demanding of care than our own.) None the less, the concern we all feel for the way in which the system of personal health-care provision deals with what we see as essential medical problems is one of the best examples of the vital role of vicarious consumption in the policy debate.

The personal health-care system generates policy problems precisely because of a conflict between 'private' evaluations that operate within the health-care market and 'public' evaluations generated by a vicarious interest in the welfare of others. The private health market is relatively efficient at providing the services that people who can afford to pay think that they want. The policy problem arises because the failure of the health market to provide health services to those who cannot afford to pay is viewed, vicariously, as a much more serious matter than the failure of the caviare market to supply caviare to those who cannot afford to pay for it.

## The Role of Doctors in Determining the Demand for Medical Services

Another special feature of the market in personal health care services concerns the role of doctors in determining the level of individual demand. Doctors, in common with many professional people, are in a position of particular market power *vis-à-vis* their consumers. Most people know when they are sick but are much less clear about what is involved in curing themselves. This is why they have to go to a doctor. The doctor tells the consumer what she needs, and the consumer is in a poor position to evaluate the quality of this advice.

This means that while illness or injury may spark off the general demand for medical services, the precise demand is formulated by the people who supply most of the services demanded. This is by no means a unique situation (garage mechanics are in a directly analogous position in relation to stranded drivers who know nothing of the workings of motor cars). Nevertheless it creates an important general distortion of market forces, particularly in a situation where the medical profession practices under a system of 'ethics' that operates to reduce competition between doctors.

When a market that deals in life-saving services is administered by professionals whose income is directly proportional to the number of these services that they can sell and who, furthermore, are not allowed by their professional association to compete directly with one another, we would expect the level of consumer demand to be kept artificially high. Some recent research has indeed shown that in Ireland doctors practising in areas where the ratio of doctors to patients is high order far more return visits than doctors practising in areas where the ratio of doctors to patients is low. In other words, the level of medical care supplied to a patient may depend as much on the need of the doctor to generate income as on the need of the patient to receive treatment.

The logic of public involvement in the regulation of such a market is identical to that of involvement in any market dealing in the monopolistic provision of an essential service. Once more, however, the essential nature of the service is a vital social variable. Few tears are shed when one of the idle rich is ripped off by an unscrupulous plastic surgeon over the removal of a wrinkle on her neck. When unscrupulous surgeons make expensive but unfounded promises to cancer victims, however, vicarious interest in the over-provision of services by the private health market increases considerably.

*Health Insurance*

Aside from the vicarious nature of our concern over the health of others, the main outputs of a personal health-care system can clearly be marketed, in the sense that they can be withheld from those who do not pay. The unpredictability of our demand for such services, together with their potentially huge cost when we do need them, means that the personal health-care system is an obvious basis for an insurance market. Given the scale of health-care expenditure in Western nations (running at almost 10 per cent of Gross National Product in countries such as the USA and West Germany), the operation of the health insurance market is likely to be a matter of considerable interest to potential consumers. Indeed, the central question of health policy in most systems can be expressed, very crudely, as one of how health insurance systems should operate.

A number of aspects of the operation of systems of health insurance generate potential policy problems. Broadly, these relate to our vicarious interest in the fate of the uninsured and to the effect on the health system of the existence of a third-party payer in the form of an insurance scheme, public or private.

Whether it is provided by the public or the private sector, health insurance shares an important feature with all other forms of insurance. It breaks the link between the person who consumes and the person who pays. This generates an interesting form of collective-action problem that can result in very high levels of health service expenditure, especially in market-based systems.

In the previous section we saw that the precise level of consumer demand for health-care services is typically determined by the suppliers, the physicians. On top of this, the existence of health insurance means that the price for specific medical services is paid not by the consumer but by an insurance company. Neither producer nor consumer has any incentive to cut costs. As it happens, insurance companies have little incentive to attempt to keep medical costs low either. Higher costs mean higher premiums; higher premiums mean higher investment income for the insurance companies even if the year-end balance on their underwriting account remains the same. Thus the higher medical costs are paid by all consumers of medical insurance, *whether or not they get sick*. Once a consumer gets sick and is told by a doctor that she needs a very expensive course of treatment that will, however, be paid for by the insurance company, she has no incentive to demur.

The collective-action problem arises because no individual insured consumer of medical services has the slightest incentive to curtail the expenses she incurs, particularly when she has been told by an expert that these will improve her health. This results in an increase in insurance charges to all. All might well prefer to agree to rack up lower charges for elaborate treatments when sick, if this resulted in much reduced insurance premiums, year in, year out. Yet no one, acting alone, can have the slightest effect on insurance premiums even by exercising the utmost self-restraint. It is significant that in countries, such as Britain, that operate a nationalized health system and are thus less susceptible to the worst aspects of this collective-action problem, recent increases in health service costs have been much lower than in those health systems that are more firmly based on private-sector insurance.

This form of collective-action problem extends to insurance in general. The particular twist introduced by medical insurance is that, if medical costs and insurance premiums were to rise out of control, people would drop out of the insurance system and thereby become objects of vicarious concern when they needed medical attention. Thus the collective-action problem of health-insurance costs commands public concern, not only because it is a collective-action problem that makes all who consume health insurance worse off but also because it contributes towards a situation in which increasing numbers of people may have to remain among the ranks of the uninsured.

There are three basic categories of uninsured, each of which generates rather different policy issues. There are those who could afford to insure themselves but choose not to do so. There are those who wish to insure themselves but who are rejected by insurance companies because they are seen as bad risks. And there are those who cannot afford to insure themselves.

The vicarious interest that we all have in the health services provided to others affects each of these categories. When people choose not to insure themselves and then need expensive medical attention that they cannot afford, our vicarious interest in their welfare will ensure that they will be treated anyway. Such people in effect save their health insurance premium in the knowledge that they can take free rides on the system should the need arise.

The issue here is one, effectively, of spillovers. The voluntarily uninsured sick generate vicarious spillovers. The policy problem is caused by the private benefits of an activity that generates public costs. The matter that is on the agenda is whether people should be allowed to run around uncovered by health insurance, given the social costs they can cause if they come a cropper. In other words, the issue is one of *compulsory* health insurance. (The arguments are thus very similar to those relating to compulsory third-party insurance for car drivers. Compulsory health insurance prevents people from being able to cause damage for which they cannot pay – in this case forcing society to pay for the cost of saving their lives.) All of this rests in practice, of course, upon the assumption that the voluntarily uninsured sick will not be left to suffer.

The argument for those who cannot afford health insurance, or for those who are denied it for one reason or another (quite possibly because they are too old or too chronically sick), takes more or less the same form. The issue that is on the table, however, concerns free (or at least subsidized) health insurance.

In each case the fact that the uninsured will not knowingly be left to die means that a *de facto* form of universal health insurance, covering those situations in which vicariously motivated action is likely, is almost always in operation. The real issue is how best to organize this market in vicarious value.

## The Framework of Health Policy

In a pure market system a problem therefore arises when uninsured people require *essential* medical treatment. If they do not have the money to pay for this, it is obviously ridiculous to say that they have chosen to die. In fact, of course, the prospective patient has no freedom of choice in such situations and cannot sensibly be seen as the decision-maker. The person with freedom of choice, the decision-maker, in such market interactions is the medical practitioner who may, of course, choose to treat the patient at below market rates. When a person is not given essential medical treatment because of her inability to pay, this is the result of a series of decisions made by private practitioners *not* to treat the patient. Given the effect of positive public vicarious interest in the treatment, this creates a justification for public action, as can be seen from Figure 3.

Figure 3 also summarizes a number of the other examples that we have used. Thus the activity of drunken driving, engaged in by those who at least *think* they benefit from it, has undisputed public health costs and is unequivocally a subject for public regulation. Smoking is an activity that generates private benefits for those who choose to smoke, yet public costs. The extent to which these social costs are traded off against private benefits depends to a considerable extent upon the context, with smoking clearly banned in some situations and allowed in others. The importation of potentially rabid animals, by contrast, invariably generates public costs much higher than will be compensated by the consequent private benefits and is an activity that is therefore subject to regulation. Most cosmetic surgery is regarded as having little public impact, positive or negative, but obviously generates considerable private benefits for some. Medical insurance, as we have seen, may well be regarded as a matter for public action when potential patients cannot, or will not, afford to insure themselves. In other circumstances the activity of health insurance will take place anyway, though it may generate collective-action problems that invite public action.

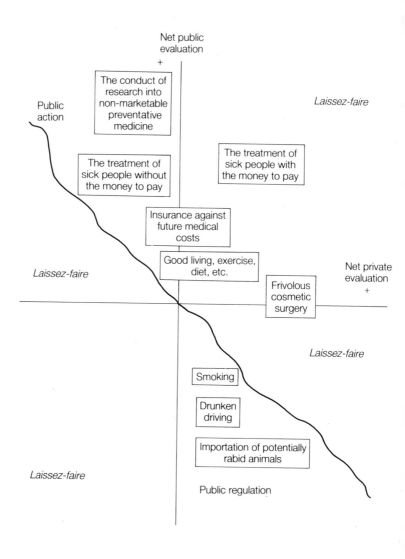

**Figure 3** Justifications for public action/regulation in health provision

All in all, Figure 3 shows that the problems of health policy in themselves cover the entire range of policy problems that we are likely to come across in the modern state. In this sense the health policy area is a microcosm of public policy in general, and most of the general forms of policy response that we are likely to encounter can be found applied to health-policy problems in most systems.

## Housing

Housing is in many ways an even more complex policy area than that of personal health care. This is largely because public and private considerations are intricately woven together into the physical and social entity that comprises a 'house'.

In order to locate various aspects of housing policy within our framework, therefore, it is necessary to consider some of the rather special economic and social properties that condition the provision of housing, whether in the public or in the private sector.

### *The Cost of Housing and the Role of Housing Finance*

Housing is *expensive*. For most people a house is by far the largest investment that they ever expect to make. Though many economists now claim that pension rights are these days more valuable than houses for many people, this counter-intuitive proposition seems not yet to have filtered through to the consciousness of the public at large. A house is certainly the most valuable *tangible* asset that most people will control.

A house is usually too expensive for most people to pay for in cash, so that they must borrow to finance either purchase or construction. This applies to all who control houses, whether private owner-occupiers or public or private landlords, and it means that the availability of loan finance is as important an aspect of housing policy as the availability of the housing itself. Without loan finance, most potential owner-occupiers cannot buy and most potential landlords cannot rent. Thus two quite separate markets are involved in housing; the market in houses and the market in money.

There is no reason why these markets should be in step with one another. High interest rates, for example, push up the effective cost of housing even when houses are not scarce. Conversely, low interest rates may counteract some of the effects of housing scarcity, at least in the medium term, if they stimulate the building of more housing. In the short term low interest rates may increase housing scarcity by boosting demand.

In general, the level of interest rates is much more volatile than the underlying supply and demand for houses. In recent years mortgage interest rates in Britain and Ireland, for example, have typically varied by 2 per cent or more around an average of 10 or 11 per cent. This has produced sudden increases or decreases in the interest cost of housing of the order of 15 per cent. An equivalent sudden increase or decrease in the capital cost of housing would be regarded as a major earthquake in the market. Thus public policy on housing cannot be divorced from that on interest rates.

Typically, housing loans are made by agencies, such as building societies in Britain and Ireland, that take short-term deposits and make long-term loans. Potentially susceptible to disastrous runs for this reason, building societies are usually very sensitive to interest-rate fluctuations, passing these on very quickly to existing borrowers. There can be little doubt that the impact of high interest rates on the housing market has acted as a constraint on the freedom of both the British and the Irish Government to accept increases in interest rates when other policy considerations might suggest these. Brave words about the free play of market forces have often been eaten in the face of the prospect of a slump in a Government's popularity among irate owner-occupiers with spiralling mortgage repayments.

An additional aspect of the market in housing finance contributes to the rather special nature of the housing market.

This relates to the nature of the loan that most people raise to finance their housing consumption. This almost invariably takes the form of a mortgage on the property. More significantly, the borrower typically puts up a rather small proportion of the total cost (say 10 or 25 per cent), while the lender makes up the balance on the basis of a secured loan. The borrower, in this way, takes all of the profits, and stands all of the losses, arising from fluctuations in housing prices. This means that housing is a very highly geared investment for most domestic consumers. In other words, if prices rise by 10 per cent, an owner-occupier who has put up 10 per cent of the price of a house doubles her money. If prices fall by 10 per cent, she loses it all.

This very high gearing of housing finance is crucial, since it exaggerates speculative aspects of the market in private houses. Indeed, it creates probably the only really speculative market in which most ordinary people participate. The key feature of speculative markets is, of course, that the level of short-term demand, and hence of prices, is determined by *expectations* of future prices as much as by any intrinsic need to consume. In other words, house prices may rise because people expect them to rise and may fall because people expect them to fall. The gearing factor greatly intensifies this process, since when I expect even a 5 per cent increase in house prices over a year, I may stand to increase my capital by 50 per cent, a rate far in excess of any other open to me in the market. Once sufficient people believe in such an increase, it becomes a self-fulfilling prophecy. Conversely, of course, expectations of falling house prices can also be self-fulfilling and can generate market collapses.

The housing market is not entirely speculative; of course, since, at the end of the day people must live in *some* house and can make only a certain level of loan repayments out of their income. But the system of mortgage finance certainly imparts a distinctly speculative flavour.

H

## The Inflexibility of the Housing Stock

Housing is more or less *permanent*. Houses last for a very long time; if they are properly maintained, they may even last for ever. Certainly, a significant proportion of the housing stock in any system has been there for quite a while. The permanency and expense of housing means that additional new houses represent, each year, a very small proportionate increase in the size of the total housing stock. (This figure is usually about 3 per cent. The total number of housing completions in Ireland in recent years has been around 26,000. Comparable figures for Britain are about 300,000 new houses added to a stock of about 20 million each year, an annual increase of between 1 and 2 per cent.) This means that major changes in the size of the housing stock in any system depends upon the effective implementation of housing construction programmes over a number of years. It also means that, in the short and medium term, the supply of housing can be taken to be more or less fixed. The import of this is that *practical housing policy is thus much more about the management of an existing stock than it is about anything else.* The scope for direct government action in response to a problem is correspondingly limited.

## The Effects of Social and Demographic Change on the Demand for Housing

We have just seen that the supply of housing is relatively inflexible. The demand for housing, however, has two quite separate components, which must be clearly distinguished in any consideration of housing policy. On the one hand, there is what we might think of as the underlying demand for housing, generated essentially by demographic and social features of the population. On the other hand, there is market demand at any point in time. This includes, in addition to the underlying demand of a given population for housing, the demand of people to change houses, to move to different types of house in different types of location and so on. As we saw in the discussion of mortgage finance, the high gearing of loan finance makes market demand potentially quite volatile.

The underlying demand for housing, by contrast, is relatively stable. The rate of change in the size of the population is small in most Western systems. The other major factor that influences the underlying demographic demand for housing is the marriage rate. Marriage is obviously the most common instigator of a demand for a new housing unit. In general terms, of course, the key variable is the 'rate of household formation', since one-parent families and unmarried couples generate a need for additional housing units in precisely the same way as do newly-weds.

Complex interactions arise in this context, since the rate of household formation may itself be determined by the state of the housing market. If prices or rents are high, couples may postpone marriage or setting up house together. If landlords or lending institutions discriminate against unmarried couples, making accommodation almost impossible for them to find, more marriages may ensue. Conversely, when housing is cheap and easy to find setting up house may become more attractive. In other words, it would be a mistake to regard the level of underlying demand for housing as something that can be read off, mechanically, from simple demographic statistics. Nevertheless, the factors affecting demographic demand are clearly *relatively* stable over a time scale of a year or so.

Considering the housing stock at any given place, however, another key demographic factor is obviously the pattern of internal migration. While houses do not move, a significant number of people must move each year, typically because of changes in employment or in their domestic arrangements. The housing market is thus very localized. There may well be a glut of housing in one place (because people, on balance, want to move away) at the same time as there is a desperate shortage of housing in another place (because people, on balance, want to move in).

Precisely how localized a housing market will be depends to an extent on transport costs. The higher are transport costs, the fewer people may be prepared to travel from one location to another, and *vice versa*. Increases in transport costs thus increase the localization of the housing market. This results in more local variation in the balance of supply and demand and, hence, in more local variation in housing costs. Higher petrol prices and a decline in public transport services have significantly increased variations in the relative prices of urban and rural houses in Ireland, for example.

National housing statistics tend not, therefore, to be very useful indicators of performance in housing policy. What matters is the provision of housing where people want it or at an acceptable substitute location. Rapid demographic changes, most commonly migration of population from country to city, can place demands on the local housing stock that, given the slow response of housing *supply*, can be very difficult to satisfy. (This, of course, is the classic Third World housing problem, which manifests itself in sprawling shanty towns around major cities.)

*Housing as a Qualitative Good*

Housing quality varies widely. Ignoring cost factors, very few people live in their ideal house. Most live in a substitute that takes into account what they are willing or able to spend on housing compared with other commodities. This has a number of consequences.

In the first place, since different people want different things, and since each house differs at least a little bit from the next, there is not a standard market price for a given house. In this sense a house is more like a Gaugin than a gallon of oil. The price that any house will fetch depends to a certain extent on finding the right person to buy it.

In the second place, everyone, by definition, is housed somewhere, even if only under a park bench. The demand for housing, therefore, is demand for houses of a certain *quality*. Even in a locality well supplied with housing, *the houses that people want* may be in short supply. The most obvious example of this can be found in the existence of long waiting lists of people who refuse to move to publicly owned high-rise apartments that are poorly designed, environmentally desolate and badly maintained. In general terms, the policy problems generated by public housing these days are typically problems of poor quality and, in particular, of aspects of poor quality that do not show up in formal statistics. Many high-rise blocks with every modern convenience have turned out to be hard to let and clearly inferior in terms of nearly everybody's standards of housing quality. What this means, of course, is that people can *feel* a housing shortage even when, on paper, there are enough houses to go around.

### Housing as an Essential Good

Housing is so essential a good that everyone must consume it in some form or another. An obvious impact of this is that vicarious evaluations are an important factor in housing policy.

A less obvious consequence is that negative spillovers of bad housing can be much more difficult to control than other spillovers. A very good example in Ireland concerns traveller encampments. If people are forced to live in caravans by the roadside, everyone is affected. Some, of course, are affected by a vicarious concern for the poor housing quality of others who do not have access to basic amenities. Others feel affected by the spillover effects that such encampments can produce. They tend not to be very pleasing in aesthetic terms; they may generate garbage if not serviced by the garbage-disposal system; and they can arouse, for one reason or another, considerable public hostility.

This is a particular example of the general tendency for poor quality housing to generate negative spillovers. It can be physically or hygienically dangerous to others. It can generate problems of demoralization, crime, vandalism and so on. People, however, cannot be prevented from living in poor quality housing if this is all that is available. Thus the fact that housing is an essential good means that the negative spillovers of poor housing cannot be regulated in the same way as the negative spillovers of non-essential activities.

## Patterns of Housing Tenure

Housing is provided in three basic patterns of tenure. In the first place, there is the owner-occupied house. Typically, this has been mortgaged by the 'owner' in order to obtain a loan covering the purchase price. There is, indeed, a very important distinction to be drawn between mortgaged and non-mortgaged owner-occupied housing. Many of the economic and social pressures that are normally assumed to bear upon owner-occupiers in general in fact bear upon mortgagees in particular. These include the effects, discussed above, of interest-rate fluctuations and of high gearing. Many retired people who own their own homes outright may, by contrast, be delighted at an increase in building society interest rates that boosts the retirement income from a nest-egg.

The differences between outright owners and mortgagees carry over to housing quality. In aggregate terms, houses that are owned outright tend to be of poorer quality than those that are mortgaged. The most recent census in Ireland, for example, revealed that the highest level of *outright* house ownership occurred in County Leitrim, the poorest county in the land, and that this was associated with the lowest levels of basic amenities such as running water, inside toilets and bathrooms. The 1981 census, however, was the first in Ireland to make such a distinction, and the full range of differences between mortgagees and outright owners of property remains to be explored.

The second basic form of tenure is the private lease. Privately rented accommodation is as heterogeneous a commodity as owner-occupied housing. It spans both the very worst and the very best standards of housing quality. However, this sector is most of all characterized, certainly in Britain and Ireland, by a distinction that has been imposed as a direct result of public policy. This is the distinction between

controlled and uncontrolled tenancies, reflecting the consequences of policies designed to realize the intimately related
objectives of rent control and security of tenure in the private
rental sector. Clearly the economic pressures facing someone
living in a protected private tenancy on a controlled rent are
quite different from those facing a tenant subject to uncontrolled market forces.

The final form of tenure arises in publicly owned rental
accommodation. This is not directly subject to market forces,
though it is subject to public policy decisions that are inevitably
conditioned by these. Most public housing, for example, is
built with borrowed money, and building costs are thus greatly
influenced by interest charges. Land, material and labour-cost
components of public housing are affected by the level of
supply and demand for them in the private housing market.
Public landlords may even decide to use public housing as a
source of revenue and may raise rents for reasons totally
unrelated to housing policy.

The balance of the three basic forms of housing tenure has
changed dramatically, in most systems, over the past fifty years
or so. One of the most fundamental changes in the housing
market this century has been the trend towards owner-
occupation. In 1914, for example, 90 per cent of British
housing was privately rented. By the early 1980s this figure had
been reduced to around 10 per cent. Over the same period the
owner-occupied sector had expanded from around 8 per cent
to over 50 per cent of the total, while the public rental sector
had expanded from around 3 per cent to over 35 per cent.

Owner-occupiers now represent an electoral majority in
Britain, Ireland and the USA, a factor that will clearly have a
bearing on likely policy developments in relation to this sector.
Perhaps the best example of the effects of the potential clout of
owner-occupiers can be found in the tax allowances that they
are typically granted to offset mortgage interest payments.
Certainly in Britain and in Ireland lip service is often paid to
the need to do away with such reliefs in the name of tax
efficiency or equity. In practice, nothing is ever done, clearly

because successive Governments have feared the effects of the subsequent electoral backlash that could be the result of abolishing the reliefs.

Obviously, policy that has an impact on one form of tenure influences others. The decline of the private rental sector has increased demand for both public rental and owner-occupied housing, while explosions in private house prices can lengthen local authority waiting lists, as first-time buyers find it difficult to get into the market.

### The Role of the Building Industry in the Supply of Housing

The building industry is a major element in most economies. Furthermore, it is an industry that tends to consist largely of small businesses. House building is not subject to anything like the oligopoly that exists in many other industrial sectors. In addition, the industry is highly speculative. Most housing developments involve considerable investments by the builder before a single house is sold. Expected movements in prices thus have a major impact on the level of activity in the industry. Thus both the *supply* of housing, as well as the *demand* for it, can fluctuate wildly on the basis of that elusive quality 'confidence'.

The building industry tends, therefore, to be very sensitive to market forces. Because of its size, this volatile industry also tends to have a significant knock-on effect on other sectors of the economy. At the very least, national unemployment levels are affected by the state of the construction industry. Employed construction workers, of course, have more money to spend on other goods, and so the knock-on effect continues. This is why the level of 'housing starts' is one of the conventional 'leading indicators' of the future state of the economy. It is also why Governments often attempt to stimulate the economy as a whole by stimulating the building industry.

### Planning Control and the Supply of Building Land

Governments almost always exercise some form of control over land development and, in particular, over the 'conversion' of land from one use to another. Such planning control, of course, has a direct effect on land prices. Huge windfall profits can accrue to those whose land is re-zoned for a more valuable use. Restricting the availability of building land can dramatically increase its value, while failing to impose strict design criteria on developers can increase long-term social costs if the occupants of substandard accommodation must be rehoused.

Whatever restrictions are applied to the use of land are bound to have a huge effect on land prices and hence on housing prices. There is a world of difference between the price of agricultural land and that of building land, and land-use planners may easily increase this difference by restricting the release of permissions for building. Conversely, housing prices can be reduced at a stroke by the release of large quantities of new building land.

What we see here is the way in which the price of building land is in part a spillover effect of the land-use planning policy that is in operation, with housing consumers paying at least part of the price for the benefits of a well planned environment. Conversely, laxer planning controls may produce uglier environments, but cheaper housing, as more building land is available.

### Public and Private Evaluations of Housing

While housing is an essential commodity, it can also represent the most extreme of luxuries. The castle, the palace and the modern-day Hollywood mansion all symbolize, after all, pinnacles of wealth and power. This makes housing a very difficult commodity to classify unambiguously in terms of a simple public versus private dichotomy.

Justifications for public involvement in housing tend to arise from our vicarious concern with the provision of such an essential good. At this basic level, despite the fact that people's views on what constitutes good and bad housing can differ quite radically, most would accept a set of 'objective' criteria that define a minimum standard of housing quality. These require a house to be dry, safe, reasonably warm and reasonably spacious and to contain essential sanitary facilities. Other important qualitative aspects of housing, such as location, design or environment, rarely find their way on to the list of the essential minimum features that form the basis of the policy problem. This may be due to the fact that explicit quantification is much more difficult with respect to design and the environment, while the usefulness of a given location depends to a certain extent on the circumstances of the occupant. (Suburban locations that are highly sought after by the affluent middle classes, for example, might be financially disastrous for the poor, who would not be able to afford associated travel costs.)

Many feel vicarious dissatisfaction when others are forced to occupy housing that does not satisfy these basic criteria, and this is the first important public component of value in the housing market.

There is also an important element of option value that people may derive from the state of the housing market. Many are quite happy to be housed where they are at a particular point in time but like to feel that they could move if they should want to do so. If, for example, the taxes on house transactions were raised to an enormously high level or if mortgage finance dried up completely, thereby rendering all moves virtually impossible, most of those who owned houses would feel a loss of utility even if they had no immediate plans to move. The same effect might be felt in the private rental sector if ferocious rent controls were introduced. The low rents and security of those with controlled tenancies could easily be more than offset by the significant reduction in the opportunity to move that would result if landlords responded to controls by taking property off the rental market.

Spillovers from housing are also considerable, though the

most obvious of these tend to be highly particular and localized. People are acutely aware, for example, of the effects of a dilapidated neighbouring house on the value of their own property. When two or three families move into a street of old houses and start renovating them, all houses in the street may rise in value. In addition to these, more generalized local spillovers are now recognized by many people. These relate in particular to crime and vandalism and often arise as a result of the *rehousing* of local communities formerly living in old and poor-quality accommodation. It is not clear whether the social costs of many rehousing programmes arise from the social dislocation of an established community or whether they are the result of the socially inappropriate and backward design and architecture of much of the new housing into which people are moved. Certainly public-sector architects now devote a lot more thought than of old to neighbourhood design.

Whatever the cause, many who are rehoused mourn the passing of their old district and the community that went with it, and this is a clear spillover effect of such policies. Beyond the very local level, the spillovers of housing are very extensive, as we have seen in the earlier sections. The state of the housing market has a major effect on the construction industry and hence on the wider economy. The market in housing finance is now an important element in the financial system of most economies.

Conversely, the housing system is itself on the receiving end of spillovers from other markets and policy areas. The level of interest rates is the product of many interrelated policy decisions and is only very marginally determined by housing policy. Land-use planning policy has effects on housing costs that are rarely analysed systematically, even if they are appreciated at a very basic level. And, most fundamentally, the general development of the economy determines underlying levels of housing demand in particular locations. In short, housing policy is conditioned in a very important way by policy decisions taken in quite distinct policy areas for quite distinct reasons.

Vicarious evaluations, option value and spillover effects all figure prominently in any social evaluation of a housing system. Despite these social costs and benefits, housing is also a very private and personal matter. While it is an essential to life, it is also a commodity on which people are prepared to spend a huge proportion of their limited resources *over and above* the provision of bare minimum requirements. Housing, of course, is intimately related to social status. Indeed, one of the way in which people often attempt to define their social status is in terms of their house. The typical response to an increase in status (resulting perhaps, from a new job or a promotion) is to move to a 'better' house.

This phenomenon has fundamental implications for public policy, since a basic element in the housing policy of Britain, Ireland and the USA has been the subsidization of various forms of private housing activity. This means that policies designed to help provide essential housing may also result in the subsidization of the consumption of housing as a luxury. The fact that a house can be anything from the most basic essential to the most vulgar expression of extreme wealth means that the subsidization of housing *in general* can have very regressive results. For example, tax subsidies to home-owners in Britain, Ireland and the USA provide the greatest benefit for taxpayers at the highest marginal rates. In other words, the biggest subsidies go to the richest. Furthermore, the evidence tends to suggest that these subsidies are used not to reduce housing costs but to acquire more luxurious houses.

The importance of subsidies in housing policy reflects a social evaluation that the private market is failing to provide enough essential housing of sufficient quality. An activity that fails the *private* cost-benefit test, in other words, is an activity deemed desirable on a *social* cost-benefit analysis. Thus the nature of the problem invites public stimulation, and this stimulation frequently takes the form of the offering of subsidies as well as the more direct response of public housing construction.

As far as the private sector is concerned, this in part reflects the reality that the very complex nature of the housing market makes it very difficult to have much of an affect on the *supply* side of things. Most crucial variables – notably the level of interest rates, the level of confidence in the industry, the market price of houses in relation to building costs and so on – are beyond effective control. At the very least, they are beyond control exclusively in the interests of housing policy. This means that policy usually concentrates on the *demand* for, and more particularly the *net cost* of, housing. The net cost, of course, can most directly be influenced by subsidies.

Such subsidies take a range of well-known forms. These include tax relief on interest payments, exemption from capital gains taxes and straight cash handouts to first-time buyers (most notably in Ireland), and they have even, in Britain, included the direct subsidization of mortgage interest rates by government. Since tax subsidies benefit only taxpayers, schemes have been devised (including the British option mortgage system and loans from the Housing Finance Agency in Ireland) to extend broadly similar subsidies to all.

Leaving aside the cost, mortgage finance tends to be more easily available, of course, to the better off. Policies aimed at extending the benefits of owner-occupation to those who are less well off have also been introduced, therefore. In Britain and Ireland these take the form of local authority mortgage finance that is made available on terms more favourable than would be available commercially to those on council house waiting lists. One hundred per cent mortgages are often offered to those who would almost certainly be rejected by building societies as bad risks. In the USA this aspect of housing policy takes the form of federal guarantees for private mortgages, achieving broadly the same effect while maintaining a lower profile for government and greater autonomy for the private sector. Government thus acts a direct provider, or at least a guarantor, of finance when this would not be provided on the basis of normal market criteria.

By and large, therefore, the important owner-occupied housing sector is encouraged by a set of incentive policies. In a situation in which quite a large proportion of owner-occupied houses would be owner-occupied with or without subsidies, the extension of *general* housing subsidies disburses resources to people whose behaviour is not changed. These people would be buying their own homes anyway and are simply given money by the Government to allow them to reduce housing costs or to increase housing expenditure. Attempts to increase the size of the owner-occupied sector have an effect only, of course, on those whose housing decisions are marginal, who would not buy a house *but* for the subsidies. There has been some attempt to concentrate policy resources on marginal groups (including, for example, special treatment for first-time buyers) or on those whose income falls below certain levels.

The basic policy puzzle posed by the owner-occupied housing sector, therefore, arises because the market in private housing is conditioned largely by those who would be consuming private housing regardless. In order to encourage more people into the owner-occupied sector, which is clearly seen as a 'good thing' in Britain, Ireland and the USA, subsidies are offered that may encourage marginal consumers but amount to free gifts to all others. This is because private owner-occupied housing straddles the boundary between public action and *laissez-faire*, with significant sectors of the population on either side of the line in each system.

The other two forms of tenure, public- and private-sector renting, tend to constitute direct alternatives to one another. Those who do not own a house and who do not have a public housing tenancy are accommodated in the private rental sector. Past policies have had dramatic effects on the *supply* of housing in each sector. For public housing, of course, government is the direct supplier. In the private rental sector, on the other hand, typical policy responses, certainly in Britain and Ireland, have been regulatory.

The private rental housing sector in Britain in particular has been heavily influenced in policy terms by the operation of a system of rent controls and by the creation of the security of tenure needed to make rent controls meaningful. This reflects a concern with the price, rather than the quality or the quantity, of private rental accommodation. Indeed, it is likely that rent controls and security of tenure have contributed to the dramatic reduction in the quantity of private rental housing in Britain. Over the past fifty years or so slum-clearance programmes that have taken private rental accommodation into public ownership, on the basis of either voluntary or compulsory purchase agreements, have reflected the main thrust of the policy response to the problem of housing quality in the rental sector. Only a relatively brief programme of improvement grants can be cited as an example of a *non-regulatory* response to the private rental housing sector in Britain.

This contrasts with the situation in Ireland and the USA, in which the private rental sector is subject to a much laxer regulatory regime. Instead, the system of tax concessions in each country operates to offer to landlords of private rental accommodation many of the tax-sheltering advantages that are available to the owner-occupied sector. In Ireland in particular such concessions (notably the now modified system of 'Section 23' tax relief) were motivated by the desire to stimulate the construction industry as much as the private rental sector *per se*. The impact on each sector, however, has been the continuation of a practice that has virtually died out in Britain, which is the building of new property specifically designed for private rental. Given that newly constructed property tends to be subjected to much stricter building controls than was faced by older property, this also has an effect, at least on paper, on the average *quality* of housing in the private rental sector.

Private rental accommodation is the market sector that must house those not provided for by other forms of tenure. At the very least, it thus forces its way on to the policy agenda as a result of our vicarious concern over the provision of essential housing for others. Subsidies for private rental accommodation, however, vary considerably in nature between systems.

To the extent that private landlords supply more accommodation as a result of these subsidies, market rents may be lower than they would be without them, and an element of the subsidy may thereby filter through the system to the tenant. Those on controlled tenancies in Britain, on the other hand, benefit from a straight imposed transfer from landlord to tenant. Considering those without controlled tenancies, regulatory policy in the private rental sector operates to increase effective demand for public-sector tenancies both by reducing the supply of private tenancies and by creating what is effectively a black market in the private sector.

To the extent that housing policy is concerned with the overall level of the supply of housing in a given area, regardless of tenure, regulatory policy cannot help. Action is needed to generate the public benefits of an activity, supplying housing to the homeless, that is not cost-effective in purely private terms. To the extent that housing policy is concerned with the management of an existing housing stock, regulation may serve to control elements of landlord behaviour that are privately beneficial yet generate public costs. In short, regulatory responses reflect a concern with *quality*, while direct action or subsidies reflect a concern with *quantity*.

Overall, however, housing policy is characterized much more than is health policy by the operation of incentive schemes and subsidies. This, of course, reflects the existence of a very highly developed private housing market in all Western systems. Policy responses, therefore, are based on government interaction with established markets, while the existing housing stock of each state represents a gigantic fixed asset that could be taken fully into the public sector only by a complete social revolution. By contrast, health policy is concerned more with ways of doing things than with fixed assets and thereby allows for a fuller range of potential policy responses.

# 12

# Conclusion

As the discussions in the preceding chapter have no doubt shown, the approach outlined in this book does not constitute a model or a theory. It makes no predictions and offers no explanations. What it offers is a method of addressing the problem. It does this on the basis of a framework built on a very broad notion of what comprises a 'rational' decision. Strictly defined, the notion of rationality is capable of generating quite rigorous models of public action. The problem with such models, however, is that their applicability in a range of different contexts is very limited. Typically, strict assumptions about the rationality of the relevant actors can be relaxed, *in a given context*, in many different ways. But if we are looking for an approach that facilitates *comparisons between different systems and contexts*, the notion of rationality must be relaxed very considerably indeed before it can be of use in this respect.

The main way in which I have relaxed conventional definitions of 'selfish' rationality has been to allow a significant role for what I have called 'vicarious' satisfactions. As I have indicated, the inclusion of vicarious satisfactions in the analysis is very much a two-edged sword. On the one hand, there can be no doubt that many aspects of the policy debate in most political systems cannot be understood without considering the ways in which people are concerned about the well-being of others. Very often these days it is some dramatic scandal, highlighting the misery of others, that breaks a log-jam in the policy process and brings about fundamental change. On the other hand, adding a dimension of rationality as fundamental as that of vicarious satisfaction almost certainly expands the notion of the rational decision so much that this can no longer form the basis of a single coherent theory. Too many things are now varying at once, something that is certainly a major price to pay for added realism.

Adding vicarious motivations to those that inform rational decision-making adds more than just a new dimension to the problem. In a sense, there is only one way to be selfish, which is to consider only yourself. By contrast, there are many, many ways to consider the welfare of others. It is this that adds indeterminacy to what could otherwise be a neat, if unrealistic, rational-choice model.

However, I hope that I have shown that there is something worth using in an approach based on a much broader notion of rationality. It does still provide us with some systematic categories within which to compare the policy evaluations of different individuals. It provides us, for example, with some indication of the implications of having short, or long, time horizons. It illustrates the effect of being risk-averse or a risk-lover. Crucially, in highlighting the distinction between evaluations made by *actors* and evaluations made by *those affected by actions*, it establishes a set of contradictions between the 'public' and the 'private' costs and benefits of a given activity. This allows activities to be located in a framework that combines public and private evaluations and provides an interpretation of different types of public response to the same type of problem.

A whole range of variables affects precise outcomes in any given situation. Two crucial categories that we have considered include the *intrinsic* properties of the various services that people demand and the various *trade-offs* that people make between various aspects of value. Such trade-offs include those made by individuals, combining direct and vicarious elements of value, and those made on behalf of a group, specifying the acceptable balance between public and private costs and benefits. Typically, the intrinsic social properties of services change with technology, while the trade-offs between public and private, or between direct and vicarious satisfaction, vary from culture to culture. If such trade-offs could be rigorously specified, of course, we would be much closer to developing a rigorous model of comparative public policy. In practice they cannot be specified rigorously, and we do much better using the policies that are actually generated to infer aspects of the relevant decision calculus in each system.

The great advantage of this approach, however, is that it imposes a degree of consistency on the analysis of policy outcomes. It does this, of course, by assuming that there is a degree of consistency in the decisions that generate the policies in the first place. But to deny this would be to deny even the possibility that public policy can be studied systematically.

# Index